illusory advice

Ngakma Nor'dzin

&

Ngakpa 'ö-Dzin

Aro Books WORLDWIDE

2015

Aro Books WORLDWIDE
PO Box 111, Aro Khalding Tsang,
5 Court Close, Cardiff,
CF14 1JR, Wales, UK

© 2015 by Ngakma Nor'dzin & Ngakpa 'ö-Dzin

The images in this book are all from photographs taken by the authors, who have transformed them into illustrations using edge-detect, threshold and invert tools.

Front cover photograph by Doc Togden.
Back cover photograph by the authors.

First edition 2015

ISBN: 978-1-898185-37-6   (Paperback)

ISBN: 978-1-898185-38-3   (Hardback)

ISBN: 978-1-898185-39-0   (ePub)

http://aro-books-worldwide.org/

This book is dedicated to our teachers,
Ngak'chang Rinpoche and Khandro Déchen,
and to all our apprentices.
Without our teachers we would have nothing to say.
Without our apprentices there would be
no reason to say anything.

Acknowledgements

It is with great gratitude that we acknowledge the correspondence and intelligent questions of our apprentices, past and present, which have formed the basis of this book.

With great respect and devotion we acknowledge the unceasing support and inspiration of our root teachers, Ngak'chang Rinpoche and Khandro Déchen, the Lineage Holders of the Aro gTér Lineage. We thank them for their confidence in us as teachers-in-training and for their affection for our growing sangha.

Special thanks must be offered to our apprentice, Ngakpa Zhal'mèd, for writing the excellent chapter introductions, and for creating the structure of the book. Our thanks also to Daniel O'Donovan for his editorial suggestions and corrections.

Ngakma Nor'dzin Pamo & Ngakpa 'ö-Dzin Tridral
Aro Khalding Tsang, Cardiff, Wales
October 2015

Contents

List of Illustrations

Editor's Preface

In the Aro gTér Tradition of Nyingma Buddhism, personal students of a teacher[1] are called apprentices. This system of apprenticeship is not unlike traditional apprenticeship in a craft or trade. Students in the Aro gTér Lineage are 'apprentice tantrikas'[2] and learn the craft of Tantra under the guidance of their teacher.

Traditional apprenticeship often entailed spending much of one's training in physical proximity to the master – sometimes living in his or her home. The apprentices of Ngakma Nor'dzin and Ngakpa 'ö-Dzin live far afield however: in Wales, in England, throughout Europe and in the United States. Much of the contact Ngakma Nor'dzin and Ngakpa 'ö-Dzin have with their students, apart from regular apprentice retreats, happens at a distance – predominantly via email.

In 2001 Ngakma Nor'dzin and Ngakpa 'ö-Dzin wrote in a letter to their sangha:

'*We would like to encourage those of you who are still electronically challenged, to obtain regular access to e-mail and the web. There is a lot of information disseminated by these means and great opportunities for communication with us and your Vajra brothers and sisters.*'

---

1 In the Aro gTér Lineage, a teacher is an ordained practitioner who is authorised to take students. Ngakma Nor'dzin and Ngakpa 'ö-Dzin are teachers-in-training
2 Tantrikas are practitioners of Vajrayana Buddhism

Nowadays, their students are distinctly less 'electronically challenged', and this has allowed the teachers to increasingly manifest teachings through digital media. Blogging, Facebook, and Blipfoto—to name but a few—have permeated their teaching style, and email has become a medium of choice when it comes to one-to-one communication with students.

One of the benefits of apprenticeship is access to an apprentice-only website. Following the example of their Lamas,[3] Ngakma Nor'dzin and Ngakpa 'ö-Dzin have posted fortnightly gDams ngag[4] on this website for a number of years. These gDams ngag are edited extracts from apprentice correspondence and contain a wealth of teaching and advice on the practice of Buddhism within everyday life. As gDams ngag, these messages are of value not only to the individual to whom they were originally sent, but to all students of the Confederate Sanghas of Aro who wish to read them. This book is a collated and edited version of this heart advice to their students.

These gDams ngag offer a glimpse into the mechanics of the teacher-student relationship. At times supportive, at times challenging, these conversations illustrate Ngakma Nor'dzin and Ngakpa 'ö-Dzin's down-to-earth and direct teaching style.

In their own words, and with the modesty that characterises them, they hope that this book can simply be an introduction to what it is like to have a Dharma[5] teacher.

---

3   The Teachers of Ngakma Nor'dzin and Ngakpa 'ö-Dzin are Ngak'chang Rinpoche and Khandro Déchen, the Lineage Holders of the Aro gTér Lineage. Ngakma Nor'dzin and Ngakpa 'ö-Dzin were Ngak'chang Rinpoche and Khandro Déchen's first students in the early 1980s.
4   gDam ngag in Tibetan is translated as 'heart advice'.
5   Dharma is the Sanskrit word used to speak of the teachings of Buddhism. In Tibetan, Dharma is chö (chos). This literally means 'as it is'.

In actual fact, it is also testimony to the skill with which they relate to both the neurotic and liberated qualities of their students.

Much has been written elsewhere of the role of the teacher in Vajrayana.[6] My hope is that this book can illustrate how this works at a pragmatic level.

The 'interruption style' in which questions are answered—and which results in emails resembling a dialogue—is a style inherited from their own teachers, Ngak'chang Rinpoche and Khandro Déchen. The effect this has on the student is not unlike the experience of relating to the teacher in person, where the student's carefully constructed mental prose is playfully dishevelled by the teacher.

Hopefully, this book will be of interest to those students of Buddhism considering entering a student-teacher relationship. I also hope it will be of interest to those students of Vajrayana who wish to glimpse how two Welsh Buddhist teachers communicate the essence of Buddhism in a manner that is relevant today.

Ngakpa Zhal'mèd Yé-rig

Paris
October 2014

---

6   See Chapter 5 'The Dangerous Friend', Wearing the Body of Visions, by Ngakpa Chögyam, Aro Books Inc, 1995.

illusory advice

1

Truth & Method

Buddhism is not a religion of truth – it is a religion of method. Its teachings are not overly concerned with expressing truth – but with methods of practice. In a sense, one could actually say that there is only one 'truth' in Buddhism: that form and emptiness are nondual.

As beginners, we start to become familiar with *form* and *emptiness* in the context of sitting meditation. We learn to experience *emptiness* as an absence of thought, that is simultaneous with presence of awareness. We experience *form* as thoughts and sensations which arise from within the condition of non-thought. We eventually begin to glimpse *nonduality* in those moments when thought and the absence of thought have the same taste. The essential practice of Buddhism is to attempt to understand *nondualilty* in the widest and most encompassing way possible, and to integrate this with every moment of one's life. Buddhism is a set of infinitely varied methods to help us achieve this.

This description of Buddhism is characteristic of Dzogchen,[1] where a particular emphasis is placed on understanding the principle and function behind different methods of practice.

---

1   Dzogchen (*rDzogs chen*), or 'total completion', is the highest vehicle in Vajrayana Buddhism. Dzogchen view presents Buddhism in a threefold manner : Sutra, the path of *renunciation* (one renounces form to discover emptiness); Tantra, the path of *transformation* (one rediscovers form from the perspective of emptiness); and Dzogchen, the path of *self liberation* (form and emptiness are experienced as nondual).

The Aro gTér Lineage, as a Dzogchen Lineage,[2] stresses the importance of understanding the different yanas [3] as varied methods of practice. Because practitioners are rarely continually at the base of Dzogchen—the realised state—aspiring Dzogchen practitioners employ whatever methods are efficacious in the moment.

These methods can originate from Tantra and, when one is not at the base of Tantra—emptiness—one will employ methods from Sutra. This weaving in and out of the different yanas— according to how one finds oneself in the moment—can be confusing because the methods may appear to contradict each other. They only appear contradictory however, inasmuch as their bases are different. At a fundamental level, Sutra—whose principle is to renounce form in order to find emptiness—could be said to 'contradict' Tantra. This is because Tantra is 'form oriented' in that it seeks to reunite form and emptiness from the perspective of emptiness.

At a more practical level, examples of contradiction are numerous. For instance, tantric practitioners will practise drinking alcohol with awareness, whilst in Sutra alcohol is strictly forbidden for monastics.

2   That the Aro gTér is a Dzogchen Lineage means that the view and emphasis in terms of practice predominantly lie in Dzogchen. Methods from other yanas will also be taught and practised according to the needs of practitioners.
3   Yana in Sanskrit, thegpa (*theg pa*) in Tibetan, is a vehicle or method of practice, and consists of a base, a path and a fruit. The base is the level of experience required to practise the yana, the path comprises the methods of the particular yana, and the fruit is the result of practising those methods.

Ngakma Nor'dzin and Ngakpa 'ö-Dzin's students come from varied practice backgrounds. Some have experience of Vajrayana, and others come from predominantly sutric traditions. For this reason many of the following dialogues are concerned with clearing up the confusion that can exist because of apparent contradictions. Some of their students come from non-Buddhist and non-religious backgrounds, and 'Buddhism as a religion' is also a strong theme throughout their teaching. Ngakma Nor'dzin and Ngakpa 'ö-Dzin state that what they teach is a religion, inasmuch as one needs to enter a view in which what one practises is 'bigger' than oneself – yet they point out how it is a religion of method which does not require faith in order to be practised.

Editor

From Sutra to Tantra

Apprentice: One of the things I've not quite taken on board fully yet is that Tantra 'allows' and works with personality. I am still influenced by a sutric view of things, even when I'm trying not to be.

Teachers: Tantra can seem rather decadent or dangerous from the perspective of Sutra. Sutra moves towards emptiness and so personality is irrelevant. Everything is calmed down. Tantra however begins with the experience of emptiness and conjures with form. Personality and the richness of life is embraced as the material with which the nonduality of emptiness and form can be discovered.

Practice is all that can be offered

Apprentice: During the last meditation group that I hosted, I was asked whether Buddhism was a religion or a philosophy. I said that although Buddhism could be seen as a 'religion' in the sense of dealing with our whole experience of living, it wasn't a religion in the sense of 'worshipping external beings'.

Teachers: Buddhism *is* a religion. It is a religion because it is always bigger than the individual and if followed there will be times when it becomes inconvenient. A philosophy is something that can be woven and adjusted when it becomes inconvenient. It is important to be clear that you are involved in a religion and it doesn't function to say that Buddhism is a 'way of life' or 'a particular psychological approach'.

As a host, it is essential to let go of any need for people to become interested in your Lineage and practice – which may be a reason to present the idea that 'Buddhism is not a religion'. You need to have absolutely no investment in anyone who attends the group wishing to take their involvement any further. You may have heard us say that if all our apprentices decided to leave and no one ever came to our sitting group, we would simply carry on practising and making ourselves available for people. All you can offer people is your practice. You can express your own feelings of appreciation for, and commitment to, your practice and Lineage, and hold a wish for others to experience the benefits you have found – but then you have to let it go and leave it up to them.

Loving Kindness

Apprentice: Is it appropriate for me to continue, on occasion, to practice other meditation practices that I learned before I became an apprentice if I feel they will help me? I was thinking of tong-len.[4]

Teachers: From the perspective of Dzogchen, any and all practices are efficacious if used at the right time and in the right way.

Practices like tong-len can be powerful, but you need to be aware that practising loving kindness on your meditation cushion, and leaving that space with a warm glow in your heart, does not necessarily mean that your anger will arise any less vigorously or immediately should you encounter an irritating stimulus.

Shi-nè[5] is ultimately more effective in cutting conditioning at the root. Through allowing spaciousness to develop in the mind, you are less at the mercy of your neuroses.

4 Tong-len (*gTong len*) is a Sutric practice, and its function is it to reduce self-orientation. When breathing in, one visualises taking into oneself the suffering of others, and, when breathing out, one gives happiness and fulfilment to all sentient beings.
5 Shi-nè (*zhi gNas*) is the Tibetan word for silent sitting. It literally means 'remaining uninvolved'. One remains uninvolved with the mind's thought processes.

Why am I doing this?

Apprentice: I have always tended to be wary of 'religion', but nevertheless wholeheartedly engaged in Buddhism because I discovered meditation as a practice with no doctrinal context. Last weekend however, during my first solitary retreat, I seemed to feel the 'religious aspect' more acutely, which caused me to experience some doubt as to why I was involved with it.

Teachers: It is a common experience in solitary retreat, that everything becomes stripped bare. One can experience moments of: '*Why on earth am I mumbling these words in a foreign language, getting up so early, and sitting on my own with aching knees and a stiff back?*' – or something to that effect. At such times shi-nè can be a great strength and support, because of its directness. The practice of shi-nè has its own logic that can be experienced directly. If other practices, such as mantra accumulation, feel less accessible at the moment, it is fine to concentrate on shi-nè.

Ritual

Apprentice: I sometimes experience quite a strong resistance to the use of ritual and symbolic form.

Teachers: You could totally immerse yourself in ritual and see what happens … or you could start to notice the rituals with which you are continually surrounded: the hello/goodbye ritual; the would-you-like-to-come-up-for-a-coffee ritual; the what-to-wear ritual for going to work, a party, a ball, or play football; the walking-towards-someone-in-a-corridor ritual; and so on. Once you start to notice the rituals of your everyday life, those which surround entering the dimension of the yidam [6] may not seem so exotic and obscure.

We know of an apprentice who felt really uncomfortable about making prostrations and tried to identify the nature of that discomfort. They realised that the aversion was due to a feeling of pride – *'why should I bow down to anyone'*. They then embarked on prostration practice privately at home, in front of a picture of their Lama. This became a powerful practice experience for them and allowed feelings of warmth and respect for the Lama to develop that they had not been able to discover previously.

---

6   A yidam *(yi dam)*, or 'awareness being', is a meditational deity. Yidams, as methods of practice, are considered symbols of our enlightened state: on engages in yidam practice as a means to transform one's neurotic mind into its liberated state.

Please grant me siddhis

Apprentice: In seven-line song[7] there is a line that is translated as 'Please grant me siddhis.'[8] What does it mean to be granted siddhis? I have always understood that we have to attain the capacity to manifest siddhis ourselves, through our practice.

Teachers: You are correct in understanding that awakening cannot be handed to you – the cause has to be created through your own effort. Through discovering the qualities of Padmasambhava by practising Dorje Tsig-dün, you can aspire to liberate the siddhis of Padmasambhava in yourself.

You effect transformation, here and now, through realising your beginningless Buddha nature—your Padmasambhava nature—and discovering that nothing is occluded; nothing needs to be added or got rid of; there is no enlightenment or lack of enlightenment. There is only the *'as it is'* of total presence.

---

7 Dorje Tsig-dün *(rDo je tshig bDun)*, or the Seven Thunderbolt Phrases.
8 'Guru pema siddhi hung' – the final line of Dorje Tsig-dün.

Addiction

Potential apprentice: Why do you not accept apprentices who smoke? Is this because smoking is looked on as 'impure' – a sutric approach? I know of sincerely practising Buddhists who smoke, yet you wouldn't accept them as apprentices.

Teachers: Smoking adversely affects the rTsa-lung [9] and hinders the arising of the benefits of meditation.

We follow our own teacher's guidance on this, just as they have followed the guidance of Kyabjé Düd'jom Rinpoche – Jig'drèl Yeshé Dorje. Please read his text on smoking. It is not that we regard people who smoke as 'bad people' – it is simply an unhelpful addiction from the point of view of practice and health. A Buddhist is one who attempts to maintain awareness rather than hiding from facts – such as the fact that smoking can kill you. Every 'sincerely practising Buddhist' will want to make the most of their human life to gain realisation – and will therefore not smoke.

If a potential apprentice felt it unreasonable to be asked to let go of such a mundane addiction in order to embrace the practice of Vajrayana, it is unlikely that they would follow our advice with regard to letting go of their addiction to neurosis. It is unlikely that we would be the right teachers and Lineage for such a person.

Potential apprentice: You do accept people who drink alcohol, yet many teachers say alcohol clogs up the subtle nervous system.

9   rTsa-lung (*rTsa rLung*): the rTsa-lung system is the subtle energetic body that is used in yogic practices.

Teachers: Firstly we would have to ask who are these many teachers, and also in what way can the subtle nervous system be 'clogged'? Having asked these questions, we would have to say that as Kyabjé Düd'jom Rinpoche wrote the 'Drinking Song' at the request of the 16ᵗʰ Gyalwa Karmapa, Kyabjé Dilgo Khyentsé Rinpoche, and Chini Lama Rinpoche, there is clearly no view of this kind within the Nyingma Tradition.

From the perspective of Tantra, alcohol has the potential to loosen the confines of our neurotic patterning – but drinking within one's limits and with awareness is always stressed. We are intoxicated with duality. Alcohol may encourage us to sober up long enough to experience a moment of direct perception.

We offer the methods of our lineage. We offer methods of practice—not truth—and it is the nature of method to differ in presentation from lineage to lineage, Lama to Lama. Method is based in view and will differ depending on view and yana. Drinking with awareness is a method of this Lineage.

Real or unreal?

Apprentice: As you know, I have been receiving counselling.
I was upset in my last session because the therapist implied that
what I perceived to be genuine spiritual experiences and ideas,
choices I'd made—even my whole sense of evolving an
understanding of my nature—were nothing more than the
fantasies of an unbalanced mind. This feedback has left me
feeling unsure about the validity of experiences I have had.

Teachers: Only you can decide whether an experience is valid or
not. Unless the counsellor is also a tantric practitioner they
cannot be expected to understand experiences that can occur in
tantric practice or during a ritual empowerment. From an
ordinary perspective visualisation practice could be viewed as
rather crazy, but from the perspective of the path of
transformation it makes sense. Tantra has its own logic and
makes sense within its own parameters.

Experiences that arise from practice are called *nyams*. The
general advice with regard to these experiences is to let them go
– they are simply an indication that you are practising. To regard
nyams as special can tend to make you want to seek them out. If,
for example, you experience a particularly strong nyam during a
meditation session—such as a feeling of bliss, or a powerful
visionary experience—there is the danger that you then start to
look for this experience again whenever you practise. You can
then turn your meditation sessions into trying to return to that
experience – forgetting that the nyam arose spontaneously
simply through your practice.

We suggest that you regard the comments of your counsellor as having been offered the opportunity to look at your experience. To reject everything you have experienced through tantric practice may be as unhelpful as believing every experience is special. Try to hold the possibility lightly that your therapist is making a valid point, whilst also holding the possibility that you have indeed had powerful experiences during empowerment and in your practice.

Apprentice: My faith has taken a real battering.

Teachers: Faith is not an issue in Buddhism. Buddhism demands the development of confidence based on gradual experience built up over time. You are quite new to practice so give things time to ferment. Keep your practice simple and light and your meditation sessions short.

It would also be useful to engage in practice that involves you physically, such as setting up shrine offering bowls, song with instruments, sKu-mNyé[10] and practice-related craftwork. Make going for a walk and enjoying the delights of the senses part of your practice. Look at things, touch things, smell and taste things, listen – and avoid conceptualising. If you are not working at the moment, get involved in activities like gardening, housework, shopping, and cooking. Volunteer for a local charity. Avoid activities that are passive like watching television, or intellectual like reading or computer work.

---

10 sKu-mNyé is a cycle of psycho physical exercises that works with the rTsa rLung system. sKu-mNyé literally means 'massage (mNye) of the subtle body (sKu)'.

Gradually your confidence will grow and you will know whether your experiences are real in that they are beneficial and moving you towards being a kinder and happier person. If the spiritual experiences you describe are making you happier, and a nicer person to be around, then this is the true test of the validity of your experience.

Drinking with awareness

New apprentice: I'm surprised that Aro gTér practitioners drink alcohol. Could you say something about that please?

Teachers: Alcohol can open our ability to be receptive and decrease our tendency to prejudice and preconception. Alcohol can loosen the restraints of our conventional view. The essence of the practice is to *drink with awareness*. Awareness can be maintained even when one is experiencing the effect of becoming slightly tipsy. The amount of alcohol that can be drunk while retaining awareness will depend on the physical capacity and practice experience of the individual.

New Apprentice: I am usually very restrained about alcohol and will strictly limit myself to one drink.

Teachers: Your restraint and self-control is commendable. It is important to only drink alcohol within your individual capacity, but it may also be useful to recognise the nature of the limits you set upon yourself. *'Is this a physiological limit so that I will become physically ill if I have more?' 'Is this a psychological limit in that I fear I will feel out of control if I have more?'*

Once you have awareness, rules are no longer necessary. It is worth challenging the limits you place upon yourself now and then, to discover whether you are limiting yourself through a rule rather than through awareness.

Carping about the animal realm

Apprentice: When you taught about animals being humourless and having their 'noses to the grindstone', I felt that you were being demeaning to spiritual creatures.

Teachers: It's important to remember that we are talking about the animal-*realm* and not about animals as such. Describing the animal-realm in this way is method – a way of understanding your own situation and states of mind.

Confusion sometimes arises through thinking that teachings on the animal-realm of the six realms [11] refer specifically to the animals we see in the world; and because of the assumption that all human-looking beings live in the human-realm. There can also be a tendency to romanticise animals, as somehow innately spiritual. Animals can display human-realm characteristics of discrimination and humour, whilst humans can display animal-realm mentality of being humourless, trapped in a particular view, lacking awareness of others. Teachings on the realms of being are helpful in enabling you to become aware of your mind-set in any moment.

Through the practice of meditation, capacity to be aware of that moment—and the realm of that moment—increases, so that 'lower realm' or 'higher realm' states of mind can be immediately exploded.

---

11 The six realms are a teaching on the nature of cyclic existence. They describe six types of conditioned existence: the hell-realm, the hungry-ghost-realm, the animal-realm, the human-realm, the jealous-god-realm, and the god-realm. The lower the realm the more intense the pain. The point of this teaching is to emphasise that even the god-realm, characterised by constant bliss, is a conditioned mode of existence that needs to be transcended. See *Transcending Madness* by Chögyam Trungpa, Shambhala 1992.

Are animals enlightened?

Apprentice: Are animals more enlightened than us? They don't seem to separate themselves from reality and so I wondered therefore whether they exist in a nondual state, reacting instantly with events as they occur?

Teachers: The directness of interaction with their environment that you perceive in animals is instinctive rather than realised. It may be useful to draw a distinction here between living in the physical form of an animal and living in the animal-*realm*. Having a physical animal form does not necessarily mean that such a being always dwells in the animal-realm. We have met horses—for example—who certainly possess a sense of humour, which would usually be regarded as a human characteristic. We have heard of animals and birds who create and manipulate tools, and of others who display acts of selflessness and kindness. Such characteristics might suggest that these animals may in fact dwell in the human-realm – at least in part.

It can be recognised that those who have the physical form of human beings can display animal characteristics: those who slavishly follow the dictates of fashion, for example, display lack of freedom of choice. Those who live their lives regimented by habitual rules, or eat with no real appreciation of taste, texture, aroma, or aesthetics, are closer to the animal-realm than the human-realm. Those who follow a sports team to the degree of having aggression towards rival supporters are living an animal-realm mentality.

Pure... impure?

Apprentice: I have a question about practice relating to one of the fourteen root vows of Tantra.[12] This is about the vow of not regarding the five psycho-physical elements [13] as impure. I have a strong tendency to regard my sensory experience very much as 'not enlightened' – somehow unrelated to practice. It is as if the psycho-physical elements are magical things existing in some 'other space' disconnected from my ordinary moment-by-moment experience. This often leads me to view my ordinary life and experience as a hindrance or obstacle to practice, which doesn't seem quite right!

Teachers: You have a background of sutric practice, so it is going to take you a little while to understand the Vajrayana perspective. To regard the body as impure—or anything as impure—is a limited and dualistic perspective.

Purity and impurity may appear as definite separate states, yet we can quite easily understand—with a little investigation—that purity or impurity are only relative definitions based in a particular view. From the perspective of Vajrayana there is no pure or impure – everything is available for transformation.

---

12 The fourteen root vows of Tantra are the central practice of any tantrika. They are vows of 'view' in that one practises viewing phenomenal reality according to the vows. At an essential level, the fourteen root vows are a dynamic description of realised mind. To practise the vows is to attempt to remain within the felt meaning of what they indicate.

13 In Sutra, the psychophysical elements are taught as the five skandhas: form, sensation, perception, mental formations, consciousness – Tibetan: Pung-po nga (*Phung po lNga*). The skandhas describe how a sentient being manifests. In the view of Sutra, liberation involves their progressive purification. In Vajrayana, however, the psychophysical elements (earth, water, fire, air and space) are considered intrinsically pure. One does not need to purify them, one simply recognises their beginningless purity.

Tantra begins with the experience of emptiness – the pregnant space from which form arises. Form is simply that which arises – and does not need to be viewed in terms of pure or impure. Human bodies are as they are and are available for appreciation. Samsara is not a separate existence to nirvana.[14] They are the same experience – it is view that changes.

14 Samsara (Skt), khor wa (*'khor ba*) (Tib) literally 'going round in circles; cyclic existence characterised by dissatisfaction. Nirvana (Skt), mya ngan 'das pa (Tibetan); state of perfection. To say that nirvana and samsara are not separate is a Dzogchen view. In Dzogchen, samsara–duality– is seen as a distortion of nonduality. As such, nirvana is discovered when we let go of our dualistic habits.

Total immersion

Apprentice: Do you think it is a good idea to focus on studying the books written by Aro gTér Lineage authors now that I am an apprentice?

Teachers: This is certainly one way in which you could approach things. It would be good to immerse yourself in the Aro gTér Lineage as much as possible. Engage with the Lineage as your chosen path so that by the end of your probationary period you will know whether the Aro gTér Lineage is your home. Certainly it is fine to read other material and attend other events, but try to attend as many Aro gTér events as possible.

The purpose of apprenticeship is to taste a unique depth of experience and involvement in a Vajrayana tradition without taking lifelong commitments. You can leap, but with the lifebelt of your probationary apprentice status.

Apprentice: I keep finding a 'but' arises for me because of my previous experience with other lineages.

Teachers: Yes we noticed on the retreat that some of your questions were not open ended, wanting-to-know-more questions, but somewhat confrontative and from an '*I think I know better*' point of view. We understand that it is confusing when you have heard teachings presented from a different perspective. The style of presentation depends on the yana from which the teacher is teaching. You are more used to a sutric presentation and now you are hearing a Vajrayana presentation.

If you hold to the familiar style of presentation as 'truth' rather than recognising it as 'method', you will close your mind to entertaining a different perspective and this will prevent you from getting to know and understand the perspective of these teachings more clearly. We are not suggesting that you suppress your enquiring mind, ignore confusion or uncertainty, or forget your previous experience – but simply that you decide to open-heartedly entertain this viewpoint for a period of time so that you can embrace the teachings of Vajrayana as we present them.

You cannot know whether you are going to really like a cake unless you taste it. If you look at it and feel uncertain, or smell it and think that it doesn't seem so good, but never actually taste it – you will never know what it tastes like. Vajrayana has to be tasted. So we would encourage you to use the probationary period to taste Vajrayana through this Lineage as thoroughly as possible. Taste with an open heart and an open mind.

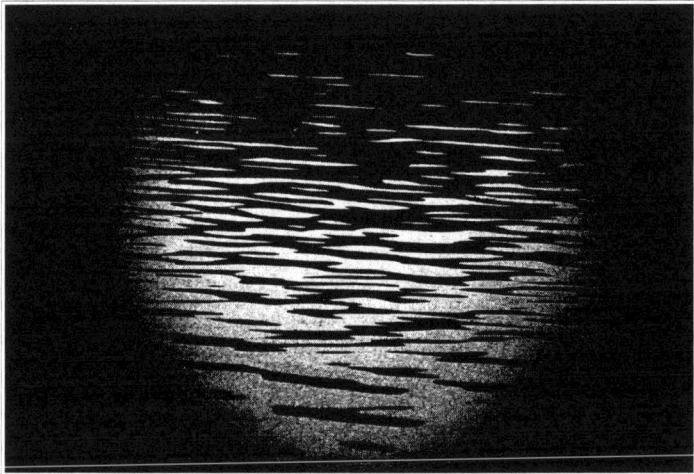

Gender becomes irrelevant

Apprentice: I have been practising seeing the phenomenal world as female [15]—including my body, thoughts and emotions—and something strange has occurred to me. If I view the totality of my perception as female does this mean that I become female? That would seem pretty strange.

Teachers: It is a Vajrayana 'fact' that men are externally form (compassion, male) and internally emptiness (wisdom, female). This is a view that is embraced in the practice of Vajrayana. It is not 'truth', it is simply the view that functions in this method.

Men view the phenomenal world as female in order to discover their occluded inner female nature. Individuals already have contact with their outer nature, so it is helpful to awaken awareness of their inner nature so that they can experience the nonduality of inner and outer. If the strangeness is disturbing, then maybe you are trying too hard and concretising the experience. If you are not disturbed by the feeling of strangeness, then do continue with the practice.

We can reassure you that you are male. This is indisputable and not something you have to discover or worry about being brought into question. Seeing the phenomenal world as your inverse gender is method. It has as part of its function the capacity to overcome habitual views of what it is to be male and what it is to be female. It liberates you to be exactly who you are.

15   This is a specific practice from the Fourteen Root Vows of Tantra.

It is not necessary to adopt a male stance to be reassured that one is regarded as male, or a female stance to be reassured that one is regarded as female. Discovering the internal qualities of femaleness for men and maleness for women overcomes the tendency to polarise experience and ignore one's inner nature. Once the nonduality of inner and outer is experienced, gender becomes irrelevant.

Rebirth

Apprentice: One Buddhist 'belief' I've never been sure about is rebirth. I find it interesting, and maybe helpful to adopt as an attitude sometimes ... but I can't say I 'believe' it.

Teachers: Sure – that is fine. Rebirth can be held as a possibility rather than as a belief. You cannot prove that you will wake up in the morning, but experience shows that this is the most likely possibility at this stage of your life, given your current level of health.

Develop an understanding of emptiness and form, perception and response, continuity of consciousness, the arising and dissolution of the elements – and it seems most likely that death is not final and total. A continuity of some description is more likely. Thus you can live with the open view of rebirth being the most likely possibility – but not as a rigid, fixed 'belief'.

Rebirth, from one life to the next, cannot be proven through your current experience. You can however, look at rebirth as the moment-by-moment experience of your life: you die and are reborn in each moment. For each new moment to arise, the previous moment has to die. 'You' die in each moment, and 'you' are reborn into each moment. 'You' are never quite the same from one moment to another, and as such, a new person arises into each moment. It is excellent to question these things and ponder on them, and the only source of certainty and confidence is your practice.

Evangelising

New apprentice: I was taught that Buddhism is right and all other paths are wrong.

Teachers: You will not be taught this by us. Buddhism is method, not truth. It is method that can be tried and tested. We have tried and tested it and found it to be entirely the right path for us – but this is not going to happen for everyone. We would not make a statement that Buddhism is the only and best path – merely that it is the only and best path for us.

We have heard that some Lamas teach that ideally, in a non-aggressive manner, the entire world should be converted to being overtly Buddhist. However the Bodhisattva vow isn't about converting beings – that would be an extreme interpretation. Liberation is the intention, and beating people over the head with Buddhism is liable to be counter-productive. Samsara does not equate to 'non-Buddhism'. In our opinion it would be better to be a happy and kind Christian than a miserable and mean Buddhist.

Vows are held internally, for oneself, and are not yardsticks for judging others. Evangelism is not part of Buddhism. Buddhism always stresses that one must work on oneself. The external manifestation is kindness, appreciation and respect towards others.

New apprentice: Among some of these zealous Buddhists, their involvement seemed to be a means to affirm their identity at the expense of others' experience.

Teachers: Sadly Buddhism can be used as a medium to develop status as much as any other club or '-ism' in which one might become involved. There are particular Buddhist personalities that can be developed, and Buddhism abounds with jargon that can become a secret language to those who know it.

We have observed new visitors to Buddhist centres being excluded by the technical conversation among practitioners, or having procedural dogma laid on them when they were too new to know what it meant.

New apprentice: I stepped back from formal involvement with Buddhism for a year because I noticed myself taking on some of the attitudes of that group – it was starting to rub off on me, so to speak, and I didn't want that.

Teachers: Well done for noticing. It is all too easy to go for the comfort of being one of the 'in crowd', adopting an 'artificial Buddhist personality', and losing touch with the heart of the teachings.

New apprentice: Unfortunately I now seem to have suspiciousness towards religious teachers, and automatically look for how they might be manipulating me.

Teachers: This is both useful and a hindrance. It is useful to have a questioning approach to any new involvement. At some point however, you will have to let go of that suspicion and relax into your involvement with the Aro gTér Lineage if you decide that this is your home. If you remain suspicious past the point of its usefulness, this will create a disconnection, and will keep you in the place of an observer.

If you find that the Aro gTér Lineage *is* your home, then you will have to make a leap of confidence and let go of suspicion, in order to fully embrace your relationship with ourselves, the teachings and the sangha.

Authenticity

Apprentice: I watched a film about Tibet the other night, and one section of the film is a wang.[16] I had never seen any footage of an empowerment before and have never experienced one from any other teacher. It was shot so you could experience it as a practice. I was so moved by it. I was able to experience—in the comparison—how I get the same experience when you conduct an empowerment. I am afraid I had very little clue how authentic our practice is.

Now I realise that previously I'd somehow thought you were doing something that might be close to how it might have been done in Tibet – but there was always a doubt or a 'but' there. I am so sorry that this must sound so rude.

Now I know that why I felt so connected, familiar and moved by the wang in the film was because you have provided me with that experience and opportunity.

Teachers: How wonderful. This is a useful thing for you to experience. There can be a tendency for people to think that because we are Westerners, and have Western teachers, that the Buddhism we practice and teach is not 'the real thing.'

We had a similar experience a few years ago when we attended teachings with Namkha'i Norbu Rinpoche. It was the first time we had ever heard anyone teach from the perspective of Dzogchen other than Ngak'chang Rinpoche.

16 A wang (*dBang*) is a Tantric empowerment.

We were completely transfixed at hearing such familiar teachings in different language, and it deepened our feelings of inspiration and devotion to Ngak'chang Rinpoche and Khandro Déchen.

Ngak'chang Rinpoche encourages practitioners to wear Western boots and hats as part of the manifestation of the gö kar chang lo.[17] The first time that one apprentice visited Nepal, they were struck by all the Tibetans wearing Western hats. When they commented on this to Ngak'chang Rinpoche he replied: *"Well did you think I made it up?"*

You will find it easier to immerse yourself in the experience of practice and Lineage from now on.

Apprentice: I have always felt grateful, but seeing the closeness of the two experiences has made me feel more grateful than ever.

Teachers: Wonderful.

---

17 Gö kar chang lo (*gos dkar lCang lo*) literally means 'white clothes, long hair'. The Gö kar chang lo is the non-celibate yogic sangha that Padmasambhava and Yeshe Tsogyel founded alongside the red, or monastic, sangha. Whereas monasticism is based on the practice of Sutra, the gö kar chang lo is based in Vajrayana.

Religion

Apprentice: I read somewhere that 'Buddhism is a religion, not a way of life.' I had always thought that Buddhism *is* a way of life, so why is it a religion?

Teachers: Buddhism is a religion of method, and that is why it appears to manifest as a philosophy or 'a way of life.' The way of living one's life *is* the practice of the religion. There are practices that are overtly religious—such as ritual practice—but a lot of Buddhist practice has to do with view – it is the transformation of view that manifests as change in behaviour and attitude. This is more subtle and all-life-encompassing than ritual practice.

Another way in which Buddhism can be seen as a philosophy or way of life, is in that there is no belief in a creator God. This differentiates Buddhism from the other major world religions, which can be a reason for some to state that therefore it is not a religion.

It is possible to trundle along as a practitioner seeing your engagement with Buddhism simply as a way of life, but inevitably there will come a time when you are confronted with the fact that Buddhism is a religion – especially if vows are taken. This is the time when the view of practice becomes inconvenient. Although your understanding of view and method clearly indicates how you should act, your self-protectiveness wants to act in a different way.

You want to indulge in recrimination, justification, prejudice, bigotry, irritation, peevishness, ignorance; you want to allow yourself to be overwhelmed, paranoid, jealous, annoyed … or whatever. If your practice is simply a way of life then you can squirm your way out of view; you can allow your own philosophy to take precedent over the demands of your religion.

It is a choice whether you allow Buddhism to be a religion or a philosophy. As a religion you have to allow Buddhism to be larger than you, and its view to be all-encompassing. You have to decide to let the needs of your practice call the shots, rather than the needs of your convenience. Then—as a religious person— you are able to become a Dharma warrior.[18]

18 Warriorship in terms of Buddhist practice refers to the idea of Pawo. Pawo is the heroic quality of one whom has no need for the illusion of firm ground. The warrior has no fear of death, because death is simply a consequence of birth.

Ignoring or accepting?

Apprentice: Buddhism seems to suggest that we ignore things that happen around us or accept them as they are. I am a little bit confused about this as this seems to be contradictory.

Teachers: We believe this may be a confusion around the difference between the sutric and the Dzogchen approach.

When life is not going quite how you expect it to go and you are experiencing difficult emotions because of this, the sutric approach would be to renounce your involvement with the emotion generated by the situation—which is regarded as negative or unskilful—and engage with positive or skilful practice instead, such as generating loving kindness. The Dzogchen approach would be to let the situation be exactly as it is and spontaneously engage with that experience – staring into the sensation of emotion.

The renunciate approach can be misunderstood as ignoring the situation, because the energy of the situation is not engaged – you step out of it in order to avoid becoming stubborn or angry, obsessive or paranoid, or falling into depression. If appropriate, you apply an antidote, such as an act of generosity when you recognise that you are being greedy or miserly. The Dzogchen approach is indeed to accept, with cheer and goodwill, that whatever way things are happening, that is the way they are happening. You wish for things to be exactly as they are. This is not passive or submissive, but a powerful affirmation of appreciation and the determination to discover nonduality through whatever arises in one's life.

2

Relationship with the Teacher

To say that the teacher-student relationship is central to Vajrayana Buddhism would be a gross understatement. In Vajrayana, the teacher *is* the practice. Methods are received from the teacher and practised under their supervision. They then validate our evolving experience. With sufficient experience of the teacher-student relationship the teacher's view begins to pervade every aspect of our lives; and so there is no sense in which the teacher's importance diminishes as one progresses along the path – quite the contrary. In many ways, the quality of one's relationship with the teacher is the barometer of one's spiritual health.

Apprenticeship in the Aro gTér sanghas is devised as a means to 'taste' the teacher-student relationship. Broadly speaking, there are two types of relationship with the teacher in Tibetan Buddhism. In Sutrayana one develops a relationship with the spiritual friend [1] and in Vajrayana the teacher is the vajra master. [2] The difference between these two modes of teaching is significant. Whereas the spiritual friend will challenge and call into question some of the student's perceptions, they will always conform to the outer conduct of Sutra, and can always be judged according to sutric criteria.

---

1   gewa'i shenyen (*dGe-ba'i bShes-gNyen*) in Tibetan, kalyana mitra in Sanskrit
2   Dorje Lopön (*rDo rJe sLob dPon*) in Tibetan, vajra charya in Sanskrit

The vajra master, on the other hand, is the teacher who can override the student's rationale, and manifest teachings that go beyond what can be judged from an 'objective' standpoint.[3] This becomes possible because the *vajra master* has a personal relationship with each and everyone of their students. This exists in contradistinction with the *spiritual friend* for whom student bodies can run into the thousands, and where a personal relationship with students is both less frequent, and not considered essential for the teachings to be transmitted.

The system of apprenticeship is one where new apprentices enter 'spiritual friendship' with their chosen teacher, and it is up to the student to decide at what pace they wish to proceed. There is the expectation that sufficient interaction will happen between the teacher and student to enable the apprentice to decide whether they feel at home with this mode of practice. This requires sufficient interaction and exposure to the teacher, which can be challenging, because the student cannot hide out. This is why Ngakma Nor'dzin once described apprenticeship as 'spiritual friendship with teeth'.

In a sense, all of the gDams ngag contained in this book could come under the chapter *Relationship with the teacher*. What is specific about the dialogues that follow is how they highlight 'spiritual friendship with teeth' and how this functions at an everyday level.

---

3   For more on this subject, see Chögyam Trungpa Rinpoche's *Cutting Through Spiritual Materialism* and *The Myth of Freedom* , Shambhala 1974 & 1976 and chapter 5 of *Wearing the Body of Visions*: 'The Dangerous Friend' by Ngakpa Chögyam, Aro Books Inc, 1995.

Many students, myself included, came to the teacher-student relationship attracted by wrathful teaching styles.[4] Ngakma Nor'dzin and Ngakpa 'ö-Dzin are by no means wrathful—quite the contrary—yet the gentle suggestions that they make when they see that something is amiss, or their subtle calling into question of some our most cherished views, has often proved too 'wrathful' for some!

Editor

---

4 A style of teaching that is concerned with directness. All necessary means are used to accelerate the student's progress – these include provoking negative emotions in students to hasten their recognition and transformation.

Keeping up appearances

Apprentice: I have observed in myself a tendency to want to tell people—especially people I respect—all the good things about myself, to get them to like me, and a corresponding tendency to want to hide the sides of myself I think people might not approve of.

Teachers: With regards to us, you can assume 'liking you' as the base camp. You can absolutely let go of any doubt on this score so that you never have to think of it again.

Apprentice: Part of me wants to hide from you my doubts and confusions and try to impress you with what a great and committed meditator I am.

Teachers: Openness will always impress us, and kindness, and a willingness to embrace change. We are not generally impressed by an appropriate display of knowledge for its own sake.

Apprentice: I am very sorry that I am sometimes rather opinionated and self-important.

Teachers: Most people have times when they are opinionated and self-important, and recognising this is half way to letting such things go. In ordinary society it seems to be generally regarded that having opinions is a sign of maturity. We would regard the openness to admit 'not knowing' and a willingness to be challenged as greater signs of maturity. Once you realise that opinions are empty then self-importance becomes irrelevant.

Scary teacher

Apprentice: I've been looking at some of the study questions about the function of the teacher, and realised that my understanding is that the function of the teacher is to scare the crap out of us! Is this right? I've been thinking that the teacher is like one of those Japanese game show hosts who find out what spooks you, such as frogs – and then sits you in a bucket of frogs.

Teachers: This would be a rather wrathful approach and we do not usually operate in this way. We certainly would not wish our students to be afraid of us. The relationship with the teacher needs to be challenging if you wish to change, but there are other aspects of the relationship. The teacher may also reflect to the student how wonderful they are – to help undermine patterns of self-deprecation. Humour and shared pleasurable experiences are all part of the teacher-student interaction. The teacher enjoys the patterns of their student's neuroses because they love the realised qualities of the student that those neuroses indicate.

Suggestions

Apprentice: I found your comments difficult to hear. I felt criticised and the need to justify my actions.

Teachers: Your letter expressed the difficulties you were experiencing. The fact that you mentioned these difficulties in a letter to us, and that you are our apprentice, seemed to indicate that you may wish us to offer suggestions.

As Vajrayana practitioners, we may be able to offer a Dharma perspective rather than a conventional perspective on such difficulties. Our suggestions were based in Dharma and on the assumption that you wished to address the situation as a practitioner. Remember, our suggestions are always just that: suggestions. It is entirely up to you whether you decide to act upon them.

You may find it useful to look at why you felt criticised. Criticism was not implied in our suggestions – just an alternative approach. You need to remember however, that criticism is not a negative thing, but rather an essential part of the work of a teacher in any field of training. The feeling of a need to justify your actions could be due to a recognition that change would be required to entertain our suggestions. Change is emptiness and form is often preferred—however unworkable or uncomfortable it may have become—rather than allowing emptiness.

Change

New Apprentice: I am conscious of the external nature of my current practice to my family life. In the process of changing oneself, how much change is internal and how much is external – such as taking a new name for example?

Teachers: There is no expectation that anyone will change their name. Some apprentices do decide to use their refuge name in all areas of life, but this is not the case for everyone. Many just use their refuge name within the context of apprenticeship, but even this is not true of every apprentice.

There's also no conveyor-belt – it's not expected that now that you are an apprentice you will automatically take ordination at some point. You set the level of involvement and intensity.

The main changes that occur to practitioners are internal. As your understanding and depth of practice increases, your view will change, and your interactions with people and the way you are in the world will reflect that change. We would like you to be comfortable … but perhaps challenge yourself a little now and then and see how it goes.

Staying in touch

Apprentice: I am sorry that I have not been in touch for such a long time and that my communications are so infrequent. The problem is that I feel that when I write to you, it should be a time of thoughtfulness and inner reflection in which I can communicate about deeper things in a meaningful and respectful way … not like dropping a chatty little comment to my mates.

Teachers: This is both correct and incorrect. Any communication is better than no communication and even short and quick messages can be meaningful. The danger with writing only when there is time for 'thoughtfulness and inner reflection' is that communication may then lack the edge of the reality of your situation – lack the immediacy of 'this is who I am now at this point in time'. It is useful for us to know you as you are with all the rough edges remaining, rather than only experiencing a smoothed and coiffured version of you.

Apprentice: Having time for such reflection seems rare – there are always more immediate things calling for my attention. The times I have set aside to write to you just get swallowed up in business and college admin, domestic stuff, or simply the need for time out and rest.

Teachers: Life is always like this. If something is important in your life then you have to consciously make time for it.

Everyday application

Apprentice: Do you think that love conquers death? That when I die I will somehow reconnect with the essence of what I love?

Teachers: Any answer would only be conjecture on our part. How would an answer help you? If we say 'yes, love conquers death' or 'no, love does not conquer death' … what difference would either answer actually make to this moment, this day, this life that is happening now? Your ability to sit on your cushion every day, to resist indulging in neurotic habit patterns, and to remain focused on being a practitioner may give you the answer in time. It is questions that address the little things that get in the way of living in pure view and engaging in practice that enable us to actually help you become or remain a practitioner on the path. It is best to be grounded in everyday practice and everyday engagement with being a practitioner attempting to live the view in your ordinary life. It would be good to focus more on ordinary friendly contact on a regular basis with your vajra brothers and sisters. Tell us about the books you have read, and the articles you have seen on one of the Aro gTér websites – and the questions this inspired. Ask us about the little things you don't understand, and the little successes and confusions that arise through practice.

Practice is like learning to walk. It may be inspiring to think of running a marathon, but when you are learning you actually have to focus on the next footstep. If all your questions relate to the marathon, there is little pragmatic help that we can offer you with regard to the next footstep.

Reflection

Apprentice: How does the teacher help a student change?
I believe I have experienced moments with you that are
transformative – when something is happening that feels quite
powerful. It feels like you are smiting distortion to the ground.

Teachers: It is not so much that the teacher is 'smiting distortion
to the ground' to effect transformation, but more that the
teacher offers the opportunity for the student to see the
situation from a new perspective and transform it for
themselves. The teacher is the catalyst or the interface that
allows the possibility of transformation. The presence and
energy to enable transformation has to come from the student.

50 ways to love your teacher

Apprentice: I am worried that I have insufficient devotion as an apprentice. I want to feel love and warmth towards you both, but it is not always there. I do not even feel anything for the yidam sometimes.

Teachers: We would suggest that you can create the circumstances for love and warmth to arise, but you cannot artificially generate devotion. You can practice appreciation and educate yourself as to the qualities of a person or yidam, but then you simply have to remain in that space and allow devotion to arise if it will.

We have known Ngak'chang Rinpoche and Khandro Déchen for many, many years. We have experienced many wonderful opportunities to feel their warmth, wisdom and kindness, to receive transmission, and to wonder at their extraordinary influence in our lives – so it is easy for us to feel devotion and inspiration whenever we think of our teachers. You have not known us for very long. Keep practising and see us as often as you can, and who knows what may become possible between us.

But do not worry – we can function as spiritual friends and Dharma advisers until—if ever—devotion arises for you.

Loving neurosis

Apprentice: I have heard it said that the teacher has to love their students' neuroses. Could you say some more about that please?

Teachers: The teacher has to delight in the potential for realisation they recognise in their students' neuroses. The teacher loves their students' neuroses without any need to be loved in return. The teacher cannot be manipulated because the teacher is not asking anything of the relationship.

The teacher does not filter what they see in their student through needing to be liked, and can therefore respond directly. In this way, the teacher is the student's greatest friend and helper in reflecting reality to the student, but also dangerous because that reflection will not always be comfortable and may be challenging.

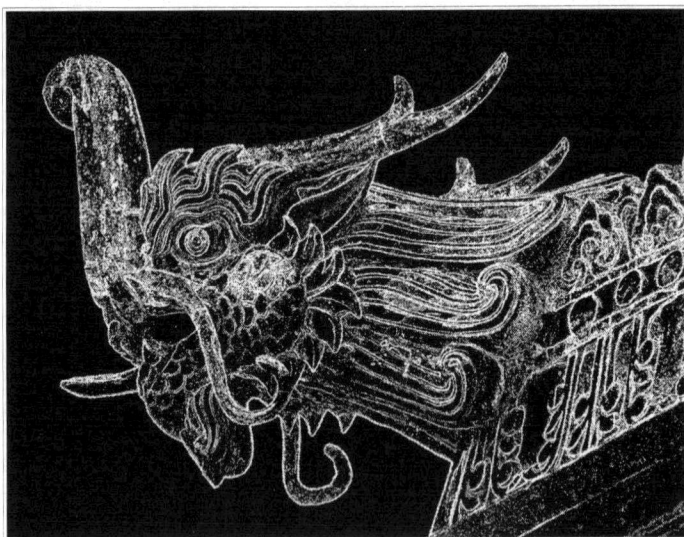

One answer for everyone?

Apprentice: I have noticed that you may tell one person that they need to practise more, and yet tell someone else to ease off and practise less intensely. I find this confusing. Can you explain why this is?

Teachers: Dharma can never be 'one answer fits all'. When you practise shi-nè you discover that your mind may go in one of two directions to avoid emptiness: dullness or distraction. If the mind is dull it needs to become more alert. If the mind is distracted it needs to settle down.

People may experience similar patterns in other areas of their life and these patterns may vary at different times in their life. You may seek oblivion in some way to avoid seeing reality, or you may distract yourself from it by being over-active in some way. In terms of practice some people may go for it flat out, full of enthusiasm and energy, but that intensity can cause problems.

They may neglect friends or family, or areas of responsibility, or they may lose touch with being a decent human being in an ordinary down-to-earth manner. Other people may need to be encouraged to put in more energy and enthusiasm else they will never get anywhere. They may also complain that they are not able to deal with life situations or feel at the mercy of their emotions. In this case more formal practice experience will be of benefit to enable them to make contact with Dharma at such times.

Visiting

Apprentice: I was wondering whether I could come and visit you next weekend.

Teachers: Certainly, that would be delightful.

Apprentice: I was a little hesitant to ask because I didn't want to waste your time. I don't have any burning questions or issues I want to discuss with you. I just would like to spend some time with you.

Teachers: It is always valuable to spend time with one's teachers just doing ordinary things together. This encourages opportunities for informal teaching and transmission to arise. This is an essential aspect of the gö kar chang lo'i dé. So please, do come and stay with us next weekend. We can chop firewood and visit the horses.

Confusion and uncertainty

Apprentice: Is it possible to enter into full apprenticeship [5] while still having confusions or uncertainties, provided there is an intention that these should be resolved?

Teachers: Confusions and uncertainties do not magically disappear once you have taken commitments. You can commit to seeing your confusions and uncertainties as an aspect of your neurosis. This is rather than holding on to them as statements of right and wrong, as reference points, or as excuses for self protection and self cherishing. It is not possible to vow to no longer be confused or uncertain! How could that be possible?

You work with your confusion and uncertainty within the context of your level of vow and commitment. If your commitment is gétrug—full apprenticeship—then you have confidence that your confusion and uncertainty—about your teachers, the path, your sangha—are able to be addressed and discussed in an open and friendly manner. You have confidence that issues can be resolved.

---

5   The first year—or up to three years—of apprenticeship is regarded as a probationary period. Apprentices who reach the end of their probationary period can then formally decide to confirm their commitment to apprenticeship, and that commitment is regarded as long term.

Isolation

Apprentice: It was lovely to be able to join you for the sangha gathering.

Teachers: We are happy that you were able to be there with us.

Apprentice: I didn't feel very connected with what was going on though. It felt as if I was observing what was happening, but didn't know how to feel involved. I don't really know why that was.

Teachers: We did notice that you did not join in with the general playfulness of the evening. This was why Ngakma Nor'dzin suggested that you have a go at the game that was being played.[6]

It was a shame you didn't seize this opportunity – instead you shrugged and said something to the effect that it wasn't your thing and didn't interest you.

It is fair enough that a game is not your usual style. However expressing that something doesn't interest you when it is being enjoyed by the general company could make those people feel uncomfortable. It also destroys the opportunity to communicate through shared experience.

Part of the practice of bodhicitta[7] is the capacity to embrace and appreciate all circumstances in which you find yourself. You could entertain the possibility of doing things that do not interest you, in order to enter into the energy of others' appreciation and enjoyment.

---

6   The game being played was 'Guitar Hero', a video game.

7   Bodhicitta, chang-chub-sem (*byang chub sems*) in Tibetan, means active compassion. In Tantra, bodhicitta relates to the energy of communication and connection.

Apprentice: Why did simply observing feel more comfortable?

Teachers: To put yourself in the role of observer is a method of controlling a situation. It is a way of attempting to deal with chaos. Not knowing your place within the situation, or being unsure of it, you stepped outside it and did not engage with it – because this felt safer than becoming involved with something you did not recognise or understand. Practitioners must embrace the charnel ground[8] of their everyday experience.

Also, we would encourage you to try and embrace our suggestions, even—or perhaps especially—when they go against your habitual patterning. Such circumstances could be great opportunities for direct experience … or at least you may find you are having more fun.

8 Charnel grounds, in ancient India, were fearful and chaotic places where unclaimed human corpses were abandoned to rot or to be eaten by wild animals. For tantrikas, the charnel ground is a practice of view where one actively embraces the chaos of everyday life situations without trying to manipulate them.

51

Comfort Zone

New Apprentice: Before I became an apprentice I had been attending Buddhist teachings for a while with a group of another tradition. One of the things that I was conscious of was the ordinariness of their approach in terms of its lack of ritual and symbol. I am aware of the comfort of that – I feel that I could have gone along to their friends' nights for many years to come and it would have been very comfortable and undemanding.

Teachers: I think we are fortunate that there are so many styles of Buddhism available to us. The different approaches make the teachings accessible to different people. Ngak'chang Rinpoche has said in the past that there needs to be room for people whose association with Buddhism is like that of people who go to church on Sunday – no more demanding than that. If that's not possible, and there is an insistence on a deeper level of involvement and practice, then the teachings may well become inaccessible for many.

We hope that you will come to feel as comfortable with the practices of the Aro gTér Tradition. It is not necessary to become involved in a lot of ritual practice. Practice can be very simple.

New Apprentice: My concern was that if I continued in this way there would be little progress – I mean progress in the sense of any change in me. I can hide from my emotions quite comfortably.

When you were teaching about emotions, I found I had nowhere to hide and that was disconcerting but also okay – if that doesn't sound too weird!

Teachers: We're glad that it was okay.

New Apprentice: It was okay, but has made me look at and question my comfort zone. It has made me feel a bit 'wobbly' about my relationship with Buddhism and practice. How 'wobbly' is it usual to be?

Teachers: There isn't really any 'usual' mode. You may have experienced some confusion and uncertainty at how our approach to teaching and practice differed from what you are used to. If it 'touched' you in some way that was helpful, then we're glad. If it has created confusion, we are more than happy to try to help with that confusion. We would say, however, that confusion is quite a good place to be because it is open, so we would encourage you to not be in too much of a hurry to stabilise your 'wobble'.

Extraordinarily ordinary

Apprentice: I would like to clarify some things regarding my relationship with you as my teachers. I have understood that it is a practice to regard you as Padmasambhava and Yeshé Tsogyel.[9] However, I've also heard you state that you are ordinary people and no different from anyone else. I find this a little confusing.

Teachers: We are teachers of Dharma – but we are not vajra masters. This is not a practice that we have suggested to you. We are ordinary people and would not expect or ask you to see us as anything beyond that. Ultimately however, every man and every woman are no different from Padmasambhava and Yeshé Tsogyel. Hence viewing one's teachers and oneself as Padmasambhava and Yeshé Tsogyel can be embraced as an inspiring practice.

If you wish to practise this view you need to be realistic about your capacity. If you are viewing us as Padmasambhava and Yeshé Tsogyel, but feel that we have made a mistake in a teaching—for example—or seem to have had a lapse in concentration, this may create tension and confusion for you. You may find it difficult to reconcile the ultimate view when faced with the relative reality of our ordinariness. However if you find what we have to say useful and illuminating, this could be inspiring *because* we are ordinary people.

---

9   Regarding the Teachers as Padmasambhava and Yeshé Tsogyel, the Tantric Buddhas, is a practice of pure view where one actively tries to see the teachers as realised beings. The function of the practice is to hasten the recognition of one's own realised qualities.

Tantra plays with ambiguities and apparent contradictions to help the practitioner escape the rigidity of their neurotic patterning. Allow this confusion to dance in your field of perception, so that you do not fix your view.

Apprentice: Would the purpose of the practice—of seeing the human qualities of my teachers but also regarding them as enlightened beings—be to help me recognise that potentiality of realisation is there for me also?

Teachers: Yes it would, but again we are not advocating it.

Enacting the role of teacher

Apprentice: What does it mean that the role of being a teacher is itself a practice?

Teachers: You cannot just suddenly decide one day that you are going to be a Dharma teacher. Enacting the role of teacher is a practice. Teachers *are* teachers by virtue of their students' commitment and devotion to them. The role is dependent on the students around the teacher.

Also remember that teachers are also students of their teachers. To learn from a Dharma teacher students need to have an attitude of openness and respect. If students view teachers as Mr or Mrs Ordinary, then their teachers are no one special for the student and they are unlikely to be able to receive inspiration from them.

Commitment and responsibility in the relationship between teacher and student is not one sided – there has to be commitment and responsibility on both sides. It is a living, interactive, creative force. When it is energised by inspiration and devotion everything becomes possible. The greatest way to test your understanding is to have to explain it to someone else. A teacher's students are an essential aspect of their practice, in the same way that the teacher is an essential aspect of practice for the committed student.

Apprentice: If the student sees the teacher as enlightened, does that then mean that it does not really matter whether the teacher has realisation or not?

Teachers: If the student develops devotion to their teacher, and can view them as an enlightened being during empowerments, then transmission is possible. The capacity and level of realisation of the teacher could be said to be actually irrelevant from the perspective of their ability to be a focus for the student's devotion and inspiration. A student may surpass their teacher in terms of their realisation, but will still maintain devotion to their teacher as the source of realisation.

The teacher functions as the vessel of transmission, as a method of reflection for the student, and as a focus for pure view. This is method. Once you are fully engaged with practice, you can experience anything and everything as a reflection of the teacher and a source of transmission and direct introduction to presence.

Realisation is not a linear progression. Realisation arises in the moment, and then may be lost in the next moment. Gaining realisation is not like ticking off the items on a shopping list – 'got that, got that, not got that … ' Transmission is possible in the moment through the power of spacious devotion. Enlightenment sparkles through—it cannot help but sparkle through because it is your endless beginningless nondual nature —and all you have to do is get out of the way of it and stop preventing the sparkling.

Is communication really possible?

Apprentice: I am very confused about myself. I seem to keep upsetting people and causing them pain. People seem to misunderstand me all the time.

Teachers: The way to let go of confusion is to practise. If you really practise then you will become a less complicated and more transparent person who is less likely to upset and hurt others.

When you look at other people, you may see that they are less greedy than you or have more generosity; less angry than you or have more clarity; that they are less compulsive than you or have more warmth and compassion; that they are less paranoid than you or have more active accomplishment; that they are less depressed than you or have more awareness. If you see this, then you can either believe that you are permanently trapped in your current state of mind, or that you can change. As practitioners we believe that we can change and that Dharma offers opportunities for change and liberation – so we practise.

Apprentice: One thing that really worries me is that we never seem to communicate very well. I think I have answered your letters beautifully and poetically, but then you reply in such a down-to-earth way that I feel you are missing the beauty of my reply and are trying to pin me down.

Teachers: That's because we are trying to pin you down. Poetry is a wonderful artistic medium, but there are times when communication needs to be simple and direct – especially now that you have expressed a desire to be considered for ordination. We suspect that your 'poetic' responses are a means of evasion – which is why we answer your letters in such a simple and direct manner.

As you are aware, the relationship between teacher and student is fundamental to Vajrayana. Within the theatre of this relationship you can become transparent to yourself, and through becoming transparent, your constricted sense of being is liberated. If this relationship is lacking—if there is no true communication, if there is no play, if there is no edge—then Vajrayana cannot function. Our communication tends to be rather stuttering – sometimes our letters meet with silence, sometimes with prevarication or often with what seems to us to be a lack of openness. If there is a lack of trust, and no sense of enjoyment of the relationship, it is difficult for anything useful to occur.

Our simple directness is an attempt to encourage you to relax into your relationship with us and allow it to really start to function. If you are able to do this then many things will become possible.

Challenge

Apprentice: During the retreat I struggled with your personalities. I realise that I struggled because I had certain needs, wants, or views which were not being met by you, but it was still disconcerting.

Teachers: We are delighted that you are able to talk to us about this. It is essential that you feel you can be 'real' about the aspects of practice that challenge you, and that you can bring to us your concerns or doubts. We are also happy with the way in which you have approached us about this.

Apprentice: How should an apprentice be when challenged by a teacher's personality?

Teachers: The most essential thing is to avoid justifying yourself and adopting a stance of solidifying your view that the teachers have a particular attitude or are behaving in a particular way. Our teachers—Ngak'chang Rinpoche and Khandro Déchen— manifest *personality display*. They may appear to be quite quixotic in how they behave with us, if they see it as a means to cut through a neurotic pattern.

Here the teacher is operating outside of our usual frame of reference, so there is no point in judging their behaviour within that frame of reference. We simply engage with the dance of the experience, even when it is uncomfortable.

Apprentice: What does it mean that the teacher can mirror the student's neuroses?

Teachers: The teacher may reply to something you have said in a particular way, or interact with you in a certain manner that reflects a quality of your presentation of yourself, so that it is laid bare for you. Alternatively the teacher may ignore the 'neurotic you' who is acting in a particular way and respond to the 'enlightened you', which you may experience as challenging or confusing. These are just examples and pointers and only hint at the possibilities.

Apprentice: I know that I would be challenged if someone wrote to me saying the sort of things to me that I write to you about. Do these questions upset you?

Teachers: No. These questions do not upset us because it is our job to answer questions. This is our role in life – our *raison d'être*.

We would always rather receive letters from apprentices that are a little direct, demonstrating that they are attempting to engage with the teachings and with practice, rather than receive 'correct', carefully worked or bland communications that hide from us.

As long as you always present your questions and concerns with ordinary courtesy and with an expectation of open communication; as long as you do not invest rigidly in your own view and allow your view to remain open and fluid – anything and everything can be discussed.

We should perhaps add a word of warning however – direct queries will tend to elicit direct replies.

Devotion

Apprentice: If devotion to the outer Lama is the tantric short path and the Lama mirrors the student's inner Lama, and the outer Lama and inner Lama are indistinguishable from enlightened Mind, how can the student develop devotion for the enlightened Mind when it is non-tangible? How does a student develop devotion for the inner Lama and how does the student do this with the outer Lama.

Teachers: Devotion to the outer Lama enables the student to be empty in relation to the Lama. This allows the Lama to conjure with the form of the student's neuroses to mirror them, so that they become transparent for the student.

An example of this would be when Ngak'chang Rinpoche made a suggestion to Ngakma Nor'dzin with regard to a building that had been vandalised. He suggested that the stone throwers were skilful in succeeding in breaking the highest windows in the derelict building. This comment completely cut through the prejudiced view she was presenting of their vandalism.

It was not that Rinpoche was condoning the vandalism, but just offering an alternative perspective. Ngakma Nor'dzin found that this opened her view so that she was then dancing with the ambiguity of whether this was a bad action or a skilful action.

If one is open to receiving transmission, then a great deal can be achieved in such moments. Huge shifts can be made in an instant. This is only possible within a relationship based on confidence in the teacher and openness in the student.

When such startling moments of transmission arise—especially in an everyday context or a casual conversation—devotion spontaneously arises in that moment as well. If the student thinks the teacher is trying to put them down by trashing their opinion, or rejects the alternative view being presented, then the moment has passed without transmission or devotion arising.

Transmission and devotion are an essential aspect of the relationship with the teacher. It is the inner teacher that receives transmission through recognising the moment and there is a warmth in that recognition.

'It is the smile of recognition as we meet our true nature face to face and discover it to be indistinguishable from the Mind of the Lama.'[10]

10   From the Aro gTér Lineage Tsog'khorlo text.

Other Teachers

Apprentice: I have discovered feelings of devotion and feel safe and unsafe with you both. As you said, Ngakpa 'ö-Dzin, the teacher is there for my enlightenment not my comfort. That is so beautiful.

Teachers: We are glad that you feel clearer about devotion and the role of the teacher.

Apprentice: Through being on retreat with another teacher I discovered it was okay to feel powerful emotions for another teacher – that I wasn't your possession, and that I could receive teachings from other teachers and this would benefit my relationship with you. I won't feel like I'm having an illicit affair when I feel something for another teacher.

Teachers: We are surprised that you had felt you were our 'possession'. We certainly don't feel that any of our apprentices are our 'possessions'. We could feel that we are the possessions of our apprentices—in that their needs dominate our lives—but we don't feel that the concept of 'possession' with regard to the teacher-student relationship is helpful.

The primary purpose of our lives is to serve the Aro gTér Lineage and in particular our apprentices. Buddhist practice emphasises personal responsibility. Although of course we feel a responsibility for our apprentices, the commitment of application remains with the apprentice. Our apprentices are adults who retain the right to listen to us or not, to act on our advice or not, to engage with the teachings and practice or not.

Apprentice: Interestingly, discovering a feeling of devotion for you both through being on retreat with another teacher, has helped me understand passionate feelings for other women whilst being in love with my partner. I do not feel so afraid of this now.

Teachers: Excellent. This is essential – to be able to have enjoyable relationships with women friends without compromising your commitment to your life partner.

Relaxation

Apprentice: I can see that it is a matter of putting what's important first and putting one foot forward at a time. Though maybe a two-footed leap can be quite appropriate at times, or even diving head first; laziness and hiding, versus effort and the willingness to expose oneself.

Teachers: This is well put. Hiding is a common problem in apprenticeship. It is not possible to have a relationship with us that will be beneficial if you hide out. There are many ways to hide out – skirting round issues we raise in correspondence; avoiding contact with us and your sangha; only bringing up 'safe' issues; only asking questions about theory rather than experience … . We have not noticed that you hide out particularly, though we feel you would benefit from being a little more involved generally.

Apprentice: Effort and exposure can be quite uncomfortable. Maybe that's why I can be a loner – then I don't have to try, put myself at risk, or do things that require effort. But the rewards of being involved with my teachers and sangha are so potentially enormous that I might as well get moving.

Teachers: Absolutely.

Apprentice: I guess that my involvement with you both has short-circuited enough of my neuroses for me to feel relatively comfortable. Now that I can dissolve myself into the void and taste the aliveness of each moment, part of me just relaxes because life has never been this pleasant.

Don't get me wrong, I have plenty of uncomfortable times where I can see my emotions going haywire, but life seems more manageable. What do you think of this rationale?

Teachers: Practice should certainly start to filter into ordinary life so that it becomes enlivened with the sparkle of emerging view. This will be uncomfortable when you notice habit patterns and neuroses, but pleasurable when you relax into view.

Retreat finances

Potential Apprentice: I would like to become an apprentice, but living on benefit it is difficult to imagine affording retreats and stuff.

Teachers: Apprenticeship is always open to anyone who genuinely wishes to engage with the teachings. There are many ways other than giving money to indicate your involvement with the lineage. There are certain expenses that cannot be avoided however – such as the food you eat at a retreat. Presumably you would have had to pay for food during the time you would be on retreat anyway, so this should not represent an additional financial burden. Other expenses can be negotiated in return for work on a retreat. This would therefore seem to leave travel expenses as the primary issue.

Potential Apprentice: You see, I have opted for an alternative lifestyle – living on the land and avoiding being trapped in a hum-drum job so that I can practice more, so it seems a shame that I cannot afford apprenticeship.

Teachers: We would ask you to consider whether living on benefits can be regarded as an 'alternative' lifestyle. It needs to be remembered that it is ordinary working people who in effect provide these benefits. There are no faceless 'powers that be' who magically provide this financial maintenance. Benefits come from the taxpayers who put up with the hum-drum jobs you are avoiding.

You are young and able-bodied and it must be asked why other people need to support you and why you believe this to be a reasonable way to live. Living in a yurt, in a simple ecological manner is a commendable choice, but it does not separate you from the millions of people who get by as best they can, trying to fulfil their own, perhaps less 'spiritual' dreams. We would encourage you to find some means of supporting yourself and your growing family, or alternatively find sponsorship of your way of life from someone who is willing to support you.

Solutions

Apprentice: I am aware that I tend to find my own solutions or ways of working with the things that arise for me, so I often have this to present you with, rather than a question. I would still, obviously, appreciate any comments from you, particularly if you would suggest a different approach.

Teachers: We commend you for working things out for yourself. Apprenticeship is expected to be an adult relationship – not a state of child-like dependence. It may however, be useful for us to hear what has arisen for you and how you approached working with that as a creative process, as well as hearing your solution, as we may have other viewpoints or approaches to suggest.

When you are working within a lineage of practice you allow the lineage to be bigger than you. Through embracing the greater view of the lineage and path of practice, you can let go of referentiality and free yourself from the limitations of your own solutions. By remaining open to the view of the teacher you can avoid defaulting to finding your own solutions preferable to the suggestions indicated by the teacher, lineage and practice. The scope of your own perspective can be more comfortable, but sometimes rather limited. Practitioners avoid going for the comfort of limited view and embrace the potentially unsettling challenge of the vastly more expansive view of the teacher, lineage and practice.

Opportunity

Apprentice: I treasure your friendship and hope that we can stay friends even if I do decide to leave apprenticeship.

Teachers: We hope that you have always found us to be friendly, but what we offer in apprenticeship is not exactly friendship and we apologise if this has not been clear. Apprenticeship offers the opportunity to enter a thread of lineage and practice that spans hundreds of years, and of which we are representatives – albeit an insignificant speck in the unfolding of that path. Apprenticeship offers the chance to enter a relationship with us as your teachers; to engage with the path of transformation; and to enter a family of practitioners. This family of practitioners will actively work to hold you in pure view and offer you the environment within which to experiment with pure view yourself. Apprenticeship offers the potential of gaining realisation.

I have to go

Departing Apprentice: Buddhism—and especially tantric Buddhism —is central to my life. It is really important to me. The problem is that I don't have time for it at the moment.

Teachers: These two statements are contradictory. If something is really important to you and central to your life then you will make time for it somehow. Do you find time to clean your teeth … to watch a film … to wash your car … to prepare meals … to do your laundry … ? The time and energy you invest in something is generally a pretty clear indication of how central it is in your life.

Departing Apprentice: I think I need to put apprenticeship on hold for 5 or 6 years. This will give me time to sort out my life and my finances. So I'd like to opt out for now and reapply at a future date.

Teachers: It would be inappropriate for us to try to dissuade you from leaving apprenticeship – that decision has to be yours and yours alone. We would ask you however to consider the 'lower key' apprenticeship options we have suggested before making a final decision. We feel that if you leave now it is unlikely that you will ever return and this opportunity will be lost.

Tantra means 'thread' or 'continuity'. It is like the thread that turns a random set of beads rolling around in a chaotic manner into a teng'ar.[11]

---

11 A teng'ar (*phreng-ba*) in Tibetan, or mala in Sanskrit, is a rosary used for counting mantra recitations.

Continuity of connection with teacher, Lineage, sangha and practice—however tenuous or limited—has power and value. It is a connection that is worth maintaining in the present, if you feel confident that you would want to have that in the future.

Departing Apprentice: I am still practising every day and intend to continue with that.

Teachers: There is little more that we would ask of any apprentice.

Thread of practice

Apprentice: There is a sense for me of how carefully all apprentices are being handled. I wondered whether this was because apprentices are reincarnating practitioners.

Teachers: We sense you feel that this is significant to you …

Apprentice: I feel that we are all wished every encouragement to return to our teachers and also feel this is something that is being pointed out as particularly pertinent to me.

Teachers: Whether you are returning to your teachers and the practice of previous lives or discovering them for the first time is actually irrelevant to your life as a practitioner in the here and now. Just practise.

Develop a relationship with your teachers and practise. This relationship will be meaningful and beneficial or it will not. Practice will be meaningful and beneficial or it will not. It would not necessarily be more meaningful and beneficial in its essence and in its lived reality through being the second time around. It may be inspiring to feel that you are part of a continuing thread of practice, but the actuality of that thread is practice in the here and now. If you continue to churn over whether this is your spiritual home, you may become so distracted from actually practising here and now, that you weaken any thread of continuity.

A problem with considering whether you are 'returning to your teachers' is that you may start to feel you are 'special'. You seem to feel the need to convince us that you are special in what you do and what you say. You are special—everyone is special—but you distort your specialness by *trying* to be special.

The Aro gTér sangha is not an arena for playing out an agenda in which one day it will be discovered and acknowledged how special you are, and Ngakma Nor'dzin and Ngakpa 'ö-Dzin will be seen as fortunate to have such a special apprentice …

3

Living the View in Everyday Life

Living the view is perhaps one of the most fundamental practices in the Aro gTér Tradition. We practise living the view to encourage the entire context of our lives to become our practice. Living the view is the interface between our formal practice and our everyday lives.

In one sense, living the view is the most advanced Buddhist practice because it means taking the recognition of the nonduality of emptiness and form—the realised state—into every moment of our existence. At a more accessible level however, we practise living the view by trying to actively recognise the infinite permutations of emptiness and form in every facet of our lives, so that everyday experience starts to reflect the nonduality of emptiness and form. It is *active* in that view needs to be cultivated and sought out. It takes energy and a dose of passion for us to remember view in our everyday lives, especially at times when our habitual tendencies are strong.

A synonym for 'view' could be 'philosophy' but that is not what is meant here. Living the view does not mean carrying around a conceptual framework with which we categorise, classify or otherwise judge our experience. Living the view is a felt experience as much as a conceptual one, and one's capacity grows through interaction with the teacher and the development of one's practice.

Living the view is central to the teaching of Ngakma Nor'dzin and Ngakpa 'ö-Dzin because everyday life and its complications are the raw material of practice. The following dialogues are replete with everyday 'kitchen sink situations'—emotional crises, relationship issues, health problems—that can all be infused with *view* when they are taken up as a practice.

Sometimes these dialogues are supportive, and point to how a slight shift in view can open things up for the student. At other times they can be confrontational when a student needs to see something directly about his or her state of mind. Apprentices can also tend to present their own opinions in the form of questions and seek a validation of their beliefs. Whatever the actual subject material however, Ngakma Nor'dzin and Ngakpa 'ö-Dzin invariably steer the questioner toward a wider and more embracing view, in which the dance of emptiness and form can be more readily appreciated.

Editor

Seeming strong

Apprentice: I somehow always give a strong impression – that's what I always hear: '*You seem so strong* … ' but I don't feel I am really that strong.

Teachers: Everyone has strengths and weaknesses, and areas of confidence and vulnerability. You seem to manifest your strength more than your vulnerability, whereas another person may tend to manifest their vulnerability more clearly. Each has its benefits and drawbacks – you might find it irritating if everyone was always trying to help you and kept checking you were alright. It sounds as though there could be a little bit of resentment there – a feeling that they should know you need help... ?

Apprentice: Yes I think that might be true. During a time when my health was a real problem, almost nobody seemed to realise it – but perhaps I did not allow people to see what was happening to me.

Teachers: We cannot expect people to know we are in need just because we feel completely raw and think this must be obvious. Everybody is dealing with their own issues all the time. 'Not asking for help' may easily be interpreted as 'not needing help'. Everyone feels they are the centre of their own little universe. If you want people to become involved in your universe, you have to invite them in – and also be willing to accept invitations.

Energy of emotion

Apprentice: The natural birth my friend had hoped for did not go as planned and in fact a cæsarian section was necessary. I felt sad about this at first, but then suddenly—and rather startlingly—found I was able to let go of this. I felt empty and receptive to whatever was happening. Is this an experience of the energy of emotion transforming? If so, what is the connection between the sadness I felt and then the sudden feeling of joyful receptiveness?

Teachers: It is always a shame when an event like the birth of a baby does not go how you would have liked it to go, but such experiences bring you face to face with the habit of living through expectation and projection rather than in the present moment. Your experience of sadness exploding into spaciousness could indeed be an experience of allowing the energy of the emotion to change of itself. The 'connection' between distracted and liberated emotion is simply the energy of *as it is.* In a dualistic, distorted relationship with energy, form is forced as an experience, ignoring emptiness. Energy does not change when you let go of manipulation, but your relationship with it changes – you are able to experience energy from the perspective of nonduality; you are able to experience the energy directly.

The boss

Apprentice: I have been trying to follow your advice on how to be with my boss. I've been attempting to demonstrate to him that I'm not afraid of him and also that I am not someone he needs to be scared of. I understood that the difficulty was how I perceived him, and not him *per se*. When I saw this I lost the fear of my boss instantly. I just feel a lot of respect and openness to this man and gratitude for working in such an exciting and interesting company. I believe his attitude towards me has changed for the better. I see now that my interactions with people are coloured by how I react and compose myself. Thank you.

Teachers: You are most welcome. You cannot give up on someone because you find them difficult to be with, and you cannot condemn them to the confinement of a pigeon-hole you have fabricated for them. By remaining open to people you always have the opportunity to approach every meeting afresh and to be continually surprised and delighted. You have now discovered this for yourself experientially and will always have this understanding to draw on when you meet other people you find difficult to get along with. The more you practise, the easier it will become. The more you practise shi-nè, the more space there is to allow such discoveries to arise, and to remember helpful experiences. We are happy that anything we have said or written has been useful, and that your relationship with your boss continues to improve.

Building a tolerance

Apprentice: I watched a film recently that explored the idea of tapping emotions as a commodity. I felt that 'only wanting to feel the good ones' was very relevant to our human experience. I am trying to build up my tolerance for uncomfortable emotions.

Teachers: Hmm ... we are not sure about 'building up a tolerance'. What does that look like? Emotions arise in the moment, abide, and then dissolve. Each and every emotion that arises is a fresh experience, so it is not possible to learn how to deal with that. Trying to learn how to 'tolerate emotions' can only ever be intellectual because actual experience is direct and real in the moment. Trying to work with emotion intellectually will not function.

The most useful practice to help cope with emotion when it arises is ... yes you guessed ... silent sitting. Recognising the movement of mind is all that can help: something arises, abides and dissolves. You get used to the emptiness of dissolution and this makes your relationship with change more comfortable. Gradually this enables you to be more present in the moment. You cannot get used to loss or pain—or disappointment, or insecurity, or any emotion—because each moment of experiencing those emotions is a new moment of experience.

You can become confident that emotion will arise, abide and dissolve through seeing that this is what always happens. Find out that this is also true of uncomfortable emotions.

Getting used to the fact that all form dissolves, makes it gradually become easier to embrace such emotions, and their arising becomes less frightening. Similarly you will feel less of a need to grasp and try to hold on to pleasant emotions, recognising that these also arise, abide and dissolve.

Worries

Apprentice: I really worry about what would happen to my dependants if I should die in an accident.

Teachers: There are certain legal and practical things that you can put in place to ensure that your dependants are cared for should you die, and this would be pragmatic and sensible to look into. Sorting these things out in this way may not set your fears to rest however, as such fears are irrational. You cannot make the possibility of bad things happening go away by worrying about them. Facing fantasy projections does not prepare you or help should such unfortunate events come to pass. You cannot control a future in which you may not be alive by living in a state of anxiety in the present. There is also the very real danger of adversely affecting the time you do have with your family by worrying about a possible projected future. It is sharing and enjoying being with your family in each and every moment of your life that is important. It is who you are for them and who you enable them to be by your presence and influence in their lives that will make the greatest difference.

Teaching

Apprentice: Occasionally people have asked me to teach them to meditate. I've tended to make vague noises along the lines of 'sometime, yeah, sure' and left it at that, rather than responding more definitely. In the past couple of months I've been asked again. What is the best approach? Should I agree and encourage their interest, or hold back a bit?

Teachers: It's always nice to encourage interest, with appropriate reticence as to your ability to teach and your depth of experience. You are not suggesting setting yourself up as a teacher, so we do not see that there is any problem in offering an enquirer some guidance. It's best to teach from the perspective of your own practice and teach what you have experienced. As you have been an apprentice for a little while now you should have some experience of shi-nè, so it should be possible for you to say something about that as a practice.

We would also suggest you say something along the lines of 'meditation' being a rather meaningless general word, and that you can only teach a specific practice – such as shi-nè. This will avoid any confusion as to what you are offering.

It may be useful to find out what the enquirer thinks meditation is and what they want – else you may launch into a profound explanation of emptiness and form and the practice of shi-nè and then discover they actually just want to learn a relaxation technique to help them get to sleep more easily.

Apprentice: I remember reading the seventh and twelfth root vows [1] and thinking that they seem to contradict one another – revealing Tantra to those who are not ready to receive it and refusal to teach those who seek instruction. Could you explain this please and tell me how I can know whether they are ready to receive it.

Teachers: There would be no problem, from the perspective of the root vows, in explaining the method of practising shi-nè. The warning about revealing Tantra to those who are not ready to receive it is to avoid putting oneself in the position of revealing practices that require transmission when transmission has not been received, or of appearing to give transmission when one is not ready or authorised to do so.

You will be aware that there are practices within the Aro gTér Lineage that are not practised on open events unless empowerment has been given – such as the mantra of Ma-gÇig Labdrön.[2] There are other practices that are only given to apprentices, and practices that are only given to ordained disciples on an individual basis. This is to protect both the practices and the practitioner.

There would be no problem about teaching shi-nè to anyone as long as you were not puffing yourself up to be a great yogi who needed to be revered by teaching it – we are sure you would not do this.

---

1   The 7th root vow is 'refusing to teach those who seek instruction', and the 12th root vow is 'revealing teachings or practices to those whom are not ready to receive them'.
2   Ma-gÇig Labdrön, a great Tibetan yogini, was the originator of the practice of gÇöd (*gcod* – often transcribed as 'chöd'). In the Aro gTér Lineage, one of the practices of Lama'i Naljor (Guru Yoga – unification with the mind of the Lama) is connected to Ma-gÇig Labdrön (*Ma gÇig Lap sGron* – 1055-1145).

Apprentice: And refusing to teach those who seek instruction?

Teachers: Again this is to do with your sense of what it means to you to be a person who can teach. If you will only teach those who you feel can benefit you in some way, but refuse to teach someone who you disdain, then your motivation is all skewed and it would be better to forget the whole thing. If you are flattered that someone has asked you to teach them meditation, and insist that they buy you lunch first, or pay your travel expenses even though you were visiting them anyway, or arrange for other people to be there at the time, and insist that they make offerings and have a throne set up for you to sit on ... you get the idea.

Relationship

Apprentice: I find that my partner is irritating me a lot at the moment and this is creating a lot of tension. I'm not sure the relationship is working out ...

Teachers: When you focus on the aspects of your partner that irritate you, that seem inconsiderate, that fail to meet your desires, or that you do not understand or like, you starve yourself and allow the relationship to wither a little. However when you focus on appreciating what you find desirable, pleasurable, interesting, exciting and enjoyable about your partner, then you are nourished by your appreciation and the relationship can bloom.

If you do observe aspects of your relationship about which you feel unhappy, it can be helpful to try to take yourself out of the focus of the feeling of dissatisfaction so that you can be more objective about the situation. When you respond with irritation it is helpful to bear in mind that the stimulus is in fact neutral. You have to *own* the irritation response, rather than blaming your partner.

Apprentice: I've been thinking that I should confront her about her lazy, thoughtless, uncaring, and distant behaviour, because otherwise I don't see how we can continue. I would like to revitalise the feelings that we had when we first got together, but don't know how to.

Teachers: A confrontational or aggressive approach is unlikely to help the situation. This is likely to produce a defensive response and close the situation down rather than opening it up.

She is who she is – and perfect from the perspective of her beginningless enlightenment. She is the person with whom you fell in love. The traits that you label as laziness, thoughtlessness, lack of care, and distance are simply her style of manifesting the confusion of samsara – that you are now noticing. During courtship you did not notice the things about your partner that conflicted with your usual patterns because your focus was on enjoying the display of your partner. Through wishing to continue to enjoy that display you enabled your partner to be more and more sparkly and beautiful.

However as soon as you change your focus to noticing that which irritates you about your partner or conflicts with your reference points, you start to diminish their ability to shine and to be a wonderful display for you. Through shutting down your openness to however your partner is, you lose their startling display and they become like trophies – shadows of their former brilliance when they were free, wild and appreciated.

Several times when we have had chats with you, you have queried whether you and your partner will stay together in the long term. While you hold your commitment to the relationship in question, and dwell on whether you really love her enough and will always want to be with her, you continually undermine what you have here and now in the present. She will sense this uncertainty and it will make her uncertain as well. If you wish to have a deep and full relationship with her, then you have to live with total conviction and commitment to that relationship in the moment.

To do otherwise is to rob the relationship of the chance to achieve its sparkling potential. You have to embrace the potency of each moment, stand by each choice, follow through on each decision – or else you condemn yourself to a life of mediocrity, diluting your experience and ability to embrace commitment and devotion.

It's your birthday and I'll cry if I want to

Apprentice: Symbolism is used everywhere and always in our lives, such as giving gifts. Is symbolism a reference-point?

Teachers: It is your relationship with something that makes it a reference-point. If it supports our neurosis then it is a reference-point. Anything can be a reference-point. Everything can be free of referentiality. It is your view that is the pertinent factor. Symbolism is everywhere in your life and is an essential aspect of your interaction with your environment.

When a friend has a birthday you wrap their present as neatly as you can, knowing that the paper is going to be ripped off – but somehow this is better than giving the present in an old paper bag. But then, why give a present anyway? Why send a card? The card, the present, and the care that you have taken over them, are symbolic of your regard for the recipient and of your good wishes. It is communicative.

Open-hearted communication is bodhicitta. If you give the present and get upset that no one noticed that yours was wrapped more beautifully than anyone else's; if you feel that insufficient applause is given to the choice of gift; if you feel that your friend moved on too quickly to their next present and did not dwell long enough on appreciating yours – then the giving and the gift were reference-points for you, complete with neurotic stickiness, and not a freely-given act of generosity, friendship and warmth.

Dreams

Apprentice: The memory of my dreams is often fresh and vivid and I have been keeping a diary of each night's dreams.

Currently I have had a series of dreams that have been relaxed and comfortable and have mainly involved asking for directions. None of them have been what I would call lucid where there has been realisation of the dream body.

Teachers: It can be useful to write dreams down as a means of developing awareness of the dream state when you wake up. However it is imperative to avoid attempting to analyse or read meaning into your dreams. Generally we are not too interested in the content of dreams, but are happy to hear of any that are especially vivid, lucid (if only in part) or particularly related to practice experience.

Apprentice: Lucid dreams may occur to me about three or four times a year. Over the past eighteen months I have dreamt of the awareness-spell of Padmasambhava a number of times.

Teachers: It is always inspiring to dream about practice. It is an indication that your practice is having an effect when it arises in your dreams, but other than that you should not read any significance into these dreams.

Panic

Apprentice: In my last email I didn't write about how badly I am getting along.

Teachers: No indeed – we are surprised to hear this as your email seemed quite happy and relaxed and you seemed fine at the retreat. Thank you for being open with us now.

Apprentice: Sometimes I get into a state where all kinds of thoughts whirl around in my head and I need all my strength and discipline not to panic. I fear that I will not be able to find my way out of this mind state.

Teachers: What do you think would happen if you did not use 'all your strength and discipline' to avoid the panic; and what would that panic look like? It sounds as though there is a fear of being trapped in this mind state so that you feel you have to fight to get out of it. Why should this mind state be any more of a trap than any other mind state? Why do you not have the confidence that it will arise and dissolve like any other mind state?

Struggle is a characteristic of samsara – struggling to make things different to how they are. The more you struggle to make things how you want them to be, the more your situation determinedly remains as it is. Try to let go of the struggle, stare at the mind-state and see what happens.

And remember – you can always telephone us.

Solutions

Apprentice: I hope you didn't mind me giving you this brief outline – it's not intended as an outpouring. I just felt that as it is such an important life issue, it was important that you know more or less what's going on for me.

Teachers: We are always happy to hear what is happening in your life – happy or sad, enjoyable or difficult.

We appreciate that you do not expect us to sort out your emotional problems and that you always take responsibility for your life, whilst remaining open to hearing suggestions and alternative viewpoints.

It is essential for a blossoming tantrika to be psychologically well balanced. Tantric practice can be unsettling and challenging, so it is important to have a good ground as a rounded adult human being before you begin. It is not the role of the teacher to 'solve' your problems, but to be a mirror that reflects openness of view. Some problems simply cannot be solved – they have to be accommodated in the flow of life. To believe in a solution to a situation is a limited view. Situations simply are as they are.

You may regard a situation as having a 'solution' from the perspective of an expected outcome. Once your expectations become empty—once you are able to let them go—situations become the beads on the thread of your life. Some beads are pretty, some are perfectly formed, some are deformed, some are disharmonious in hue – eventually you are able to appreciate the qualities of all and any bead.

Surfing

Apprentice: Everything feels mediocre at the moment – my practice, my relationship. I wish I could always feel like I feel on our retreats. I wish my relationship was as amazing as it was when we first got together when it was like riding a wave of ecstasy. I wish those intense moments of inspiration I lived in when I first began to practise were always there. Why does it all have to become mundane?

Teachers: You are something of a romantic and a passionately idealistic person. There is a yearning in you and a desire for the ecstatic embrace of realisation. However it can be that in yearning for the goal you forget that the journey is not separate from the goal. A long-term relationship cannot realistically be an unbroken wave of fantastic sex, dreamy-eyed fascination with one another and unspoken intuitive knowing of each other's being. Practice cannot always be vivid and intense. However, the breaking of the wave can also be an ecstatic experience, as can the quiet stillness of the ocean when there are no waves. Each aspect of experience has its qualities to be discovered and appreciated. As a practitioner you can learn to dwell in the emptiness and form of each new moment of every day, so that nothing is ever experienced as mundane or mediocre. Through yearning for what might be, fretting about what isn't and worrying about what is, there is the risk of missing the vibrant, sparkling possibility of each moment.

Fantasising

Apprentice: I seem to fantasise quite a lot and I don't always enjoy it. Sometimes they take me off in directions I don't want to go – for example sometimes I find myself thinking I could just push someone or do something unpleasant and it worries me that such thoughts arise.

Teachers: Everybody has fantasies, scenarios that play out in the mind, which they would rather not experience. Their nature is connected to their karmic tendencies as individuals.

The good news is that they are also connected to the intrinsic energy of enlightenment. Some people have wild sexual fantasies, some have violent ones. This is not in itself anything to worry about as long as you do not act on the impulse.

Apprentice: Sometimes they are about bad things happening in my life. Often I feel amused that such a strange thought should have come to mind, which I think is probably quite a good thing ... ?

Teachers: It is useful to look at what you are getting out of your fantasy projections – do you feel that by fantasising the worst, the worst will somehow be avoided; do your fantasies provide a screen preventing genuine open interaction? Finding them funny is certainly helpful. This suggests a lightness and openness in relationship to the fantasies. Blocking them will not make them go away and may create convoluted emotional states. Mostly we would suggest you let them go and do not indulge them. Let them go in the same way that you let go of the content of mind when practising shi-nè.

Apprentice: What would be the karmic effect of my fantasies?

Teachers: Karma is perception and response. You create patterns that colour your perception, which affect your response, which further colours your perception .... . A complete karma is when you intend to do something, you do it, and you are satisfied that you have done it. If you indulge conjuring the fantasy, engage in the fantasy, and are pleased with the experience, then you have patterned yourself to do it again.

If you fantasise committing an unskilful action, such as violence towards someone, imagine enjoying the action and feel satisfied that it has been enjoyable, then you have patterned your perception to some extent though not as strongly as if you had actually committed the act. It may be that you are not aware of deciding to have the fantasy because it is too fast – phhhtt! You are just in there.

Try to engage with the energy of the fantasy, rather than the conceptual content of the fantasy – stare at it in the same way that you would stare at an emotion. Then interesting things may start to happen, and the compulsion of fantasy creation will begin to lose its power. As with dreams, the content is ultimately irrelevant. It is the energy of the experience, and what we do with that energy that is pertinent.

Health

Apprentice: I have been experiencing some strong health symptoms lately and have been feeling quite sorry for myself. This does not feel like an appropriate response for a tantrika – although it's not my reaction most of the time. Most of the time it's okay—'that's how it is …'—and I recognise everybody has got something …

Teachers: Yes everybody has got something, but that does not mean it should be ignored. In fact your 'somethings' are your greatest opportunity for practice.

Apprentice: I recognise that I am lucky not to have a really serious problem—like an actual disability—but even these niggling health problems seem to dominate my life at times. This is how I am experiencing it at the moment.

Teachers: As these are symptoms that you have experienced throughout your life, it may be that these are 'ornaments' of this life—qualities of this body—and therefore have to be accepted as part of who you are.

We are not suggesting that you accept them in a resigned, suffering manner, but in a celebratory way. These symptoms are an aspect of who you are in the same way as your hair colour, body type or fingerprint. If you are in actual pain, then this certainly needs to be addressed, but other less aggressive symptoms can be embraced.

Give yourself the time and space to make friends with your symptoms. They are part of who you are. They may feel like an extra factor that is tagged on to your life and that you would rather like to be rid of but if this has not proved possible so far, then continuing to battle with them is not likely to suddenly start to be successful. If your attitude is always one of wishing to separate yourself from these symptoms, then they will tend to increase in significance in your mind and figure even more strongly in your kyil'khor.[3]

If you yearn for them to become empty they will become more and more form. It is like when you go on a diet – food becomes the focus of your day: counting calories and exercise points; deciding what you can or cannot eat … it becomes disproportionately important.

Perhaps you could have a 'symptoms retreat' where you allow yourself to fully engage and acknowledge whatever is arising and stare at the sensations and emotions that accompany the symptoms for a few hours or a day – or however long feels workable. It may be interesting to see what happens when you simply sit with these symptoms rather than trying to get along despite them. Perhaps you have struggled on for so many years trying to ignore these health problems and put them aside, that occasionally they come and whack you across the face demanding not to be ignored any longer.

---

3 Kyil'khor (*dkyil 'khor*), mandala in Sanskrit, means 'centre and periphery'. At an individual level it is one's entire physical, emotional and intuitive experience of being – an experience that can be dualistic, or nondual. One is simultaneously at the centre of one's own khyilkhor, and at the periphery of others' kyil'khors.

Awareness and control

Apprentice: If a person loses control and hurts somebody, but remains aware of the situation, then surely that person has not really lost control?

Teachers: This sounds like either an intellectual and hypothetical question or a vague personal question. If it is a personal question it would be helpful to have more specific information about the situation to which you refer

However, let us look at what you are saying.

We would agree that if there is awareness of a situation in which harm is possible, and the instigator continues with their actions, then there is no loss of control, as any action would be undertaken knowing what was happening. So—for example—if you see an opportunity and jump ahead in the queue, but do this knowing that it will make the person who was really next in line wait longer, then you have decided to indulge your selfishness knowingly and inconvenience the other person.

However your ability to let go of selfishness and engage in honourable activity depends upon: an awareness of the situation; the capacity to cooperate with awareness so that the need to protect or benefit the 'me project' is dissolved; and the further capacity to follow through with the kind and honourable action.

A lack of capacity to engage at the second stage and let go of protecting or benefiting yourself, could be regarded as loss of control in a sense.

This is because you are falling into the pattern to which you have been conforming for so long that it clicks in automatically before you are aware of it. Through practice, loss of control in this sense can be undermined. From the perspective of karma, a complete karma requires intention, the act, and satisfaction about the completion of the act. Hence if there is awareness (intention) and somebody gets hurt through the action, whether or not it is a complete karma will depend on whether the instigator is satisfied that someone got hurt. If they are not and regret that there was harm, then this is not a complete karma.

Tantrikas are all always responsible for the results of their actions even if those results were unintentional. If someone has been hurt through your actions—whether or not there was intention, self-control or awareness—you remain responsible for the outcome and should try to help the person who has been hurt.

Life is practice

Apprentice: I keep asking myself how do I build Buddhist practice into a life that is already overflowing in a way in which it doesn't just become another demand or pressure to be managed?

Teachers: The style of practice in the gö kar chang lo is that life is practice. Practitioners find time to engage in formal sitting practice because it feeds and expands their capacity to engage in everyday-life as practice.

You have been a practitioner for a few years now, so it should have become possible for you to have gained some experience of this. If your practice has become 'another demand or pressure to be managed' then something has got lost for you.

Apprentice: I worry that it is often weeks or even months between my letters to you, but as I sit here giving time to writing to you now, I am aware of at least eight other tasks I ought to be doing or want to do, at least five people I am letting down by not attending to their needs … It also feels like this when I try to find time to sit.

Teachers: We are sorry that writing to us has become a worry. Short notes are always acceptable – or you could telephone us. It is always possible to find time for short periods of formal practice – especially if one's practice has become a potent force of change in one's life and a source of the development of openness and kindness.

A solid life

Apprentice: I am practising on a daily basis now, but my morale is very low. Practice helps a lot, but it does not change my situation of not having a job and being lonely. I used to live a solid life back home – everything was planned and followed a sort of pattern. Here nothing is solid and nothing is predictable. I keep wondering why I left my other life.

Teachers: When we talked about your plans to emigrate, you may remember that we suggested that your feelings of dissatisfaction with living at home and your expectations of a new life were unrealistic. You are now able to appreciate what you had, which was not appreciated before you left it. You now know that moving the pieces of your life around does not bring happiness. Your projection—the rosy view of what you thought life would be like in your new country—has not materialised.

We are sorry that you are having a difficult time, but happiness may arise in any situation – it is not dependent on circumstances. Happiness and satisfaction are inner qualities that arise through living in the moment. Look on this as a great opportunity. Laugh at the projections and expectations you imagined, and embrace the situation as you find it.

Take responsibility for where you are, and conscientiously avoid recrimination and blaming others for the difficulties you are experiencing. You are most fortunate that you can return to your parents' home if it finally becomes irresolvable. So enjoy the time that you are there.

gTér-bum

Apprentice: I have a gTér-bum[4] that I would like to bury in a particular place where contractors ripped up the countryside to build a road. There are a group of us who campaigned against the road construction. I wondered whether it would be all right to do this and whether you would come and perform a ceremony.

Teachers: There are a couple of things that would need to be considered here. Firstly: who owns the land and would they be happy to have a gTér-bum buried there and a ceremony performed? The second is the principle of the gTér-bum as a treasure vase that is of benefit to all beings – not just to the faction that you happen to support.

Bearing these factors in mind, the gTér-bum would need to be buried with an openness of view that it will help all those connected with the new road. It will help renew the land, people and wildlife that were disrupted through the road work.

It will be of benefit to those who wanted the road to be constructed, the people who drove the JCBs and worked on the road, and to the people who now use the new road. The principle of the potential benefit of a gTér-bum extends beyond time, place and philosophy.

---

4 A gTér-bum (*gTer bum*) is a 'treasure vase'. It is a 'treasure' in that it is traditionally filled with precious and consecrated substances. gTér-bum are used to bless or heal physical locations. As such, they can be buried in the earth, sunk in the foundations of a house, or simply kept in one's home.

Every gTér-bum is to be placed, buried or submerged with the intention of benefiting everyone and everything, everywhere, without any sense of limitation as to what that benefit might be or any partiality in the distribution of benefit.

We don't wish to misjudge the views of your friends. An ecologically-minded attitude can be of benefit, but as you know from the teaching on the five precepts, you can never separate yourself from others, nor adopt the attitude that your ways are inherently better or that you are 'purer' than others.

The gTér-bum cannot be buried with any hint of divisiveness, such as any idea that it is 'for' the campaigners and 'against' the construction firm, the government who funded it, or the motorists. The principle of gTér-bum is beyond that and will benefit people long into the future – people who may speak a language you don't understand, build buildings you don't like and do all manner of things of which you may disapprove.

Looking good

Apprentice: Why is presenting ourselves smartly so important? Isn't how we look irrelevant to practice?

Teachers: You have a responsibility to those with whom you are practising to assist them in every way possible in the practice of pure view.[5] Any way in which anyone undermines others' ability to enter this practice is unacceptable, and contradicts the basic precepts of practice which we all attempt to live within.

When you attend an empowerment you are entering the presence of Padmasambhava and Yeshé Tsogyel and presenting yourself smartly is a sign of respect and appreciation. When your physical presentation is an expression of not bothering to be clean, tidy and smart you are failing to enter the compassionate activity of the bodhisattva path. For the bodhisattva the sensibilities of others are never irrelevant or insignificant. The bodhisattva regards the experience of others as real and takes responsibility. The bodhisattva attempts to help others to be peaceful and comfortable in their thoughts, emotions and reactions wherever possible

Vajrayana embraces form. Form is actively appreciated in all its multifarious manifestations. Practitioners enjoy their instruments, caring for them and making bags to protect them. They appreciate the manifestation of other beings and objects around them, and delight in their beauty.

---

5   Pure view is a practice where one actively tries to see others as realised beings.

When a practitioner buys something, they buy the best that they can afford. When they eat, they eat what they enjoy rather than simply to stuff their faces. They delight in the experience of form through their recognition of its transience and the preciousness of its temporary manifestation.

This is also true of personal form – the practitioner cares for their body and the clothes that adorn it as a compassionate communication with the world.

Misconception

Apprentice: I have come to realise that I have a lot of suppressed anger. I am trying to root out the suppressed anger via investigative autobiography, acceptance of hurt, release, and forgiving.

Teachers: In Vajrayana the method is not so much rooting out and releasing, as recognising emotional patterning and allowing it to transform into its natural, non-distorted state. Recognise when you are suppressing emotion and stare at it rather than trying to push it down.

Apprentice: This is making me ever more aware of the Four Noble Truths and strengthening my desire to end suffering.

Teachers: That is a generous response to the recognition of your own state of patterning.

Apprentice: Aversion, indifference and suffering seem to come into play a lot as well. It seems that you can't have one without the others also being present. Whatever has a top has a bottom, if you distort the top you distort the bottom and the sides – am I making sense?

Teachers: This is an unusual threefold grouping: aversion, indifference and suffering. The three root misconceptions are attraction, aversion and indifference and these create the experience of dissatisfaction (or suffering).

It is addiction to assessing all experience on the basis of these three that leads to the creation of reference points, and to grasping for solidity, permanence, individuality, continuity and definition.

People live by: '*I like it, I don't like it, or I don't care about it*' or: '*give me more of that because it supports my view of myself in some way; keep that away from me because it threatens my view; or I don't care about that because it neither supports or threatens my view.*'

These three can be understood as inseparable, because the mindset that has attraction will inevitably have aversion and indifference as well. If there is a reference point for what is attractive this also becomes a reference point for what will create aversion and indifference – and so on.

Apprentice: So the way forward is to stay in the present moment, act not react, and achieve the nondual state?

Teachers: Staying in the present moment is certainly essential. Whilst dwelling in duality, action and reaction will both be dualistic. It is necessary to discover the moment of nondual awareness before intention or perception arise.

The wrong letter

Apprentice: I spoke to my friend for a couple of hours last night. We discussed my letter. They told me that they had been wandering around the park in shock.

I feel bad that I inadvertently caused them such distress. I fear that I may have to live with the repercussions of this letter for a long time to come.

Teachers: Ngak'chang Rinpoche once told us a story. He was travelling with a lady who had experienced a difficult situation with a friend. During the journey she wrote a letter to her friend and showed it to Rinpoche and asked him what he thought of it.

Rinpoche said, "*It's a clear well-written letter. It expresses what you feel – but how do you wish your relationship with your friend to be after she receives your letter?*" The lady said that she would like to be better friends. Rinpoche replied, "*Don't send that letter, then.*" She asked Rinpoche why, as he had said that it was clear, well-written, and expressed what she felt. Rinpoche answered, "*There are various factors to be considered when writing such a letter: what you want to say; what you feel should be said; what you think the person needs to hear; and finally – what the desired outcome might be. The final factor is the one you have to bear in mind. If you don't care what the outcome is – send the letter. If you do care, then you had better re-write it.*"

In any situation there are several letters that could be written. There is the letter that tells the recipient how you feel about the situation. There is the letter that tells them what you want them to hear.

You could write a letter than pacifies the situation without reference to your feelings, or the letter that is expressive without concern about their feelings. What is important however is knowing what you wish to achieve when you write to someone and having the capacity to feel how a letter will be received and whether it will achieve that desired outcome. For example, whatever the right or wrong is about a situation; a wish to remain friends is unlikely to be met if your letter is full of accusation and recrimination.

You sent your friend the wrong letter this time – and everyone has done this at some point in their life. Your friend is willing to talk this through with you so there is reason to hope that the situation is redeemable. It sounds as though your friend cares about you enough to keep the lines of communication open. Be happy about this and build on it – and let go of the regret that you got it wrong this time.

Interesting times

Apprentice: Albert Ellis used to get his clients to replace thoughts like 'that's terrible', 'that's awful', 'that's tragic' with 'that's inconvenient'. I found this an enjoyable and helpful game to play with myself.

Teachers: That is an intriguing idea. Our only comment is that it tends towards *re*-programming rather than *de*-programming. Sometimes things *are* actually terrible, awful or tragic, and then it is best to acknowledge that.

Apprentice: Things have been a bit 'inconvenient' here lately.

Teachers: We are sorry to hear that. It could be seen as an aspect of good-hearted intent to avoid panic, over-reaction or harmful emotional outbursts, to regard your life circumstances as 'interesting' when they are 'inconvenient'.

There is the danger however, that this simply becomes a way of trying to make everything smooth and feel safe. Tantrikas try to ride the energy of chaos without attempting to smooth it over or make it feel safer.

Apprentice: It was *interesting* trying to get a flight on Good Friday to go and help my mother, when everything was shut and also discovering that my passport had expired a year ago.

Teachers: We see that you have spotted that the word 'interesting' can be used in the same way you describe using the word 'inconvenient', but it may be better to tell it as it is. It must have been distressing that your mother was taken so ill while on holiday abroad.

It must have been frustrating that it was so difficult to get a flight. It must have added considerably to the worry of the situation to find that you did not have a valid passport. It is actually more real to say that the situation was frightening, worrying, frustrating, crazy, difficult, hard work … Tantrikas call a spade a spade, whilst still recognising that their opinion that the spade is a spade is empty and dualistic.

Apprentice: She is now home and doing well but facing major surgery in the summer.

Teachers: We are glad that you were able to deal with the situation and that she is recovering.

Apprentice: With three out of four of mine and Sarah's parents now on the endangered species list and a fourth doing his best to put himself there, the next year could be... *interesting*...

Teachers: It will be what it will be and we are sure that you have the capacity to work with it as best you can.

4

Being a Practitioner in the World

Being a practitioner in the everyday world is a source of inspiration but also a great challenge. As tantrikas, we aspire to be changchub sempas.[1] *Changchub sem* means active compassion, and 'pa' (an abbreviation of pawo – *dPa' bo*) means warrior. The changchub sempa therefore, is the *awakened mind warrior* we aspire to be, where the 'war' we wage is that of developing kindness and openness.

The warrior-like quality of the changchub sempa comes from their intimacy with death. Death is not feared because it is seen as being simply the natural outcome of birth. This knowledge is what makes the warrior fearless, and this fearlessness gives them the freedom to act without the crippling effects of self-protective referentiality. The warrior is simply open to what is and sensitive to the needs of others.

Living in the world as Buddhist practitioners is like living on the changchub sempa's battlefield. In battle, warriors attempt to react impeccably to whatever presents itself. They need peripheral vision because battle is a 360° affair. Warriors will do whatever needs to be done because that is their commitment; this is how they have decided to live their lives.

It is impossible to relinquish warriorship, or decide to fight only half the battle. The changchub sempa wages war on duality for the benefit of all sentient beings.

1   *byang chub kyi sems pa*

For this aspiration to be meaningful and workable, it needs to be connected to the everyday experience of life. How can an office worker carry this commitment? What does it mean for a nurse to be a warrior?

Being a practitioner in the world is connected with how we live in the world as tantrikas. In a sense, the dialogues here are not so dissimilar to those of the last chapter, *living the view in everyday life*. Here however, they are more concerned with how we manifest in the world: the professions we choose, the career options we take, the family choices we make.

Because the Aro gTér tradition is a householder tradition— where practice and everyday life are inseparable—practitioners need to earn a living and engage with working life. Apprentices come from all walks of life and manifest a rich variety of occupations. What is made apparent in the following gDams ngag is that whatever a student's chosen profession, the same questions arise. What truly qualifies as right livelihood? Is work in the corporate world damning in some way? How can the apparently uncaring and less pleasant aspects of work be dealt with?

As a working couple having raised two children, Ngakma Nor'dzin and Ngakpa 'ö-Dzin are intimate with the complexities of professional life, and encourage students to take a wider and more appreciative view of their circumstances.

A recurring theme concerns the practice of the 84 Mahasiddhas of ancient India.

These practitioners came from all walks life and counted, among others: thieves, businessmen, prostitutes and hunters. They achieved realisation by using their everyday occupations *as* their method of practice – something that all students of non-monastic Buddhist traditions can look to as an inspiration.

Editor

Work

Apprentice: I have just discovered that my partner is pregnant. It has made me realise that I want to be able to provide a decent home life for my family. I've wasted so many opportunities and given up good jobs – now I need to settle down. I've started looking for something that I can really make a go of. I don't want us to be living on benefits all our life. Unfortunately because I've always kicked against the system, I don't have much to offer and will end up doing some menial job probably.

Teachers: It is useful to reflect on the mistakes one has made in the past and on the experiences one has gained. You have had a lot of useful experiences, from what you describe, and these can all be helpful in your wish to move on from there. It shows strength of character to respond so immediately to the responsibility of the pregnancy. We would encourage any apprentice to try to be self-supporting. We are not keen on people living on state benefit in order to *do their own thing*, so we are glad to hear that you would like to find a way of supporting yourself and your family. Any employment, even if it appears menial, can have its own purpose, and can bring a real feeling of self worth and achievement if approached as a tantrika.

Apprentice: Perhaps I can start at the bottom and work my way to the top, to be someone, and then laugh at it all.

Teachers: You are someone wherever you are and whatever you are doing. The most valuable 'someone' you can ever be, is simply a kind person with honour and integrity.

If you have these qualities then you are a bodhisattva warrior, whether you are cleaning out a toilet at the time or heading a board of directors. Remember the Mahasiddhas. They numbered amongst them people of all walks of life, who discovered realisation through doing whatever it was they were doing exactly as it was.

Whose turn is it?

Apprentice: I really enjoyed your examples of irritation, such as 'squeezing the toothpaste tube in the middle' and 'whose turn it is to unpack the dishwasher.'

Teachers: Good. It's often helpful to have simple examples.

Apprentice: I don't know whose turn it is to unpack the dishwasher. I suspect it is mine, though I unpacked my mother's dishwasher this morning. Is it impossible to take turns at unpacking? Maybe it's no one's and everyone's turn?

Teachers: Indeed. We have enjoyed your light-hearted play with this topic. If the job needs doing and you are able to do it, then why should you want anyone else to do the job? The *khandro-pawo nyid-da mélong gyüd* [2] teaches that when making love the khandro and pawo focus on the pleasure of their partner rather than on whether their own pleasure is being satisfied. Similarly you can focus on whether you can do a job rather than relying on others to do it in their turn, because of the pleasure you experience through saving them the work.

There is a story of beings trying to eat using forks with incredibly long handles. In nirvana this works because everyone is enjoying feeding each other. In hell it is great suffering because everyone is trying to feed themselves and so the long-handled forks become a desperate encumbrance. [3]

---

2   The khandro-pawo nyid-da mélong gyüd (*mKha' 'gro dPa' bo nyi zLa me long rGyud*)is a teaching where romantic relationship becomes a spiritual practice. See *Entering the Heart of the Sun and the Moon* by Ngakpa Chögyam and Khandro Déchen, Aro Books Inc, 2009.

3   This story is attributed to an itinerant preacher, Rabbi Haim of Romshishok, Lithuania.

The perfect parent

Apprentice: I am becoming more and more excited by impending parenthood – a whole new adventure. I am aware however, that it is severely challenging to my 'I just want to be a yogi in a cave' head-trip and also makes my 'walking around the world' dreams look even more distant

Teachers: You may not have to let go of all of your dreams, but you will need to consider whether being a parent can accommodate them without harm. The path of the Mahasiddhas is to live life exactly as it is and to enable that to be the path of realisation. Being a parent offers many opportunities for practice. You could become the 'perfect parent' and discover realisation through that as a method.

Right livelihood

Apprentice: I have to decide which course I'll be taking this year.
I have a number of choices. Neuroscience is very appealing, but
it raises many questions about the use of animals in research.
Things are improving, but is it better to keep back from such
ethical hotspots, or to put yourself in a position where you could
perhaps influence things? Have you any thoughts, from your
knowledge of living as practitioners? Are there any things I
should bear in mind while I'm making my decision?

Teachers: You are at an interesting crossroads. For a practitioner,
choices need to be based on a realistic assessment of one's
personal capacity—the capacity to help and to be of benefit to
others—and one's need to have a livelihood.

We are all always compromised. Being alive is the cause of
discomfort or death for other beings. Every time you cook, drive
your car, walk across a lawn, take medicines, etcetera, etcetera,
you are causing the death or discomfort of other beings.

It is not possible to live in the world 'purely'. Your life is the
cause of suffering for other beings. Everything is
interconnected. Practitioners recognise their dependence on all
other beings, in their ability to live their lives. They try not to do
harm and to be of benefit to others within their capacity. Your
decision needs to be based on whether you feel able to carry the
responsibility of known acts that may be required of you.

It is true that much can be achieved in changing attitudes within a sphere, which would be harder to achieve by campaigning from the outside. This idea however, needs to be tempered with the reality of your actual activity on such a course. It would be a difficult path for a Buddhist who holds to the wish to avoid harm, to follow a career that involved actually causing harm. It is not possible to live as a practitioner and opt out of such responsibility.

If you use medicines that had animal testing as part of their production, you are part of and responsible for their experiences in that process.

If you eat meat, you are responsible for that animal's death. You can sing Dorje Tsig-dün before eating, and practice tsog'khorlo[4] to renew your wish not to harm others and to try to benefit them.

To actually be the person who slaughters the animal, injects the animal, performs the surgery, or sets up the experiment, is extremely real and direct. To remain open and aware in such a profession would require a highly developed practice. To have practitioners in such areas could be most beneficial to the animals concerned, but the potential for benefit would need to be considered against awareness of the real capacity of the practitioner.

4   *tshogs kyi 'khor lo* – Ganachakra in Sanskrit, ritual feast.

Baby you can drive my car

Apprentice: I am faced with what appear to be two opposites in my life. My job requires me to be involved with fining people for traffic offences and I see that people suffer from the penalties and fines they incur. Buddhism teaches me that I should be compassionate and not cause people unhappiness – so this has caused me to feel something of a dilemma.

Teachers: You have to live within the context of the society in which you find yourself, and abide by the laws of that society. If you do not, life becomes difficult. If you wish to drive a car, then you have to abide by the rules and regulations that surround that responsibility. If you choose to ignore those rules and break them, then you have to expect to suffer the results of that decision. This is the responsibility of driving a car.

Apprentice: Yes, that was the only way I could come to terms with it – that I was not really interfering with anyone's life as I was not the one who chose to break the law. I feel that if people break these traffic laws, it shows that they are being irresponsible and disrespectful to others.

Teachers: This may be true, but there could be many reasons why a traffic regulation is broken. It may be that someone does consciously decide to drive faster than the speed limit, for example, or it could just be due to a lapse of concentration. It could be a lack of awareness of the speed limit in a particular place, or confusion about the layout of a junction. People drive when they are tired, or ill, or in a rush, or with a car full of unhappy children … people make mistakes.

Apprentice: Yes, I see that.

Teachers: It is not necessary to take on the assumption that they are being irresponsible or disrespectful to other drivers, to justify to yourself the requirement to award a fine. If this is your job, then you have to do your job. You are not responsible for the unpleasant outcome an individual suffers who breaks known laws, or their response to that. However you do have control over how you respond to them. You can be friendly and sympathise with them. You can be caring towards them if they are distressed or having difficulty paying the fine. The important thing is to avoid becoming thick-skinned – not caring about the inconvenience or hardship of those penalised, or dismissing it as their own fault and thus not worth thinking about.

Understanding that the individual is responsible for their actions does not mean that you cannot care about the discomfort that results from that action. Within the limits of your professional responsibilities, you can help those with real difficulty paying a fine to be aware of any help available to them and means of appealing.

Even those who are belligerent and angry are worthy of a kindly response, because—as a practitioner—you recognise that they harm themselves by compounding their ingrained patterning with an angry and aggressive response.

If you continue to find that you are uncomfortable with the responsibilities your job demands, in the end you may have to consider whether it is the right career for you.

Worthwhile pursuits

Apprentice: Should all Buddhist practitioners be engaged in 'worthwhile' careers – such as in the caring professions or working toward peace and the relief of hardship in the world? I feel that ethical work and lifestyle is very important and that we should all be working to stop the spread of the power of the multinational companies.

Teachers: You could dedicate your life to feeding the hungry, housing the homeless, stamping out child abuse, ending all war, healing the sick, comforting the dying … there are innumerable good causes in which it could be worthwhile to become involved.

Any such venture however, would have to be entered into for the satisfaction of the effort of the day-to-day work itself, rather than for any vision of the ultimate success of the project.

Spiritual practice is a worthwhile cause that can succeed. The path is valuable and the goal is achievable. Only spiritual development steps outside the mere manipulation of the form of your existence. Only spiritual development can give lasting liberation and freedom from the dissatisfaction and hardships of samsara. It is important to free people from suffering in its most physical and gross form and give them comfort, so that they can discover the subtleness of dissatisfaction in the context of the comfort and pleasure of their lives. Then they have the opportunity to engage in spiritual practice. But it is important to be realistic about how much you can achieve.

Dying with dignity

Apprentice: Is it considered to be better to allow someone to die with dignity or to strive to keep them alive a little longer but in a state of increased suffering?

Teachers: The state of mind is the most important aspect of dying. It is important to die with an alert and happy mind so that it is an alert and happy mind that enters the bardo state between rebirths. The length of life in that sense is irrelevant as the mind-stream simply continues. It is the capacity of the mind to be present and aware in the moment that either moves your consciousness in the direction of greater openness or greater confusion. If there is the potential for greater clarity and peace of mind through prolonging someone's life, then it is likely to be worthwhile. Strong painkillers may dull the mind however, and physical pain may unsettle the mind. So if there is the likelihood of prolonging life leading to increased confusion and dullness of mind, then it may be of little benefit.

Won't you buy me a Mercedes-Benz

Apprentice: The people I work with only seem to want to be able to afford an exotic holiday or to live like pop stars. I wouldn't mind those things as well, but feel as a practitioner I should be doing more to help others.

Teachers: Indeed. As practitioners it would be inappropriate to indulge in regretting having insufficient money to fulfil fantasies, such as going on exotic holidays or owning expensive cars as one might if one was a pop star. Practitioners understand that such things are irrelevant to the cause of satisfaction. They practice rather than feeling sorry for themselves.

They regard the unhappiness of others as real and to be taken seriously – whatever form that unhappiness takes, but are realistic about their capacity to help people, about their opportunities to help, and about what might be the most valuable focus of their lives. The most valuable focus in a practitioner's life may be helping the person who sits at the desk next to them in the office of a multinational company.

Through being a Dharma warrior you can help ordinary people in everyday situations. If you can work for an organisation whose purpose is to help with the suffering in the world, that is all well and good, but still your most valuable contribution may be your influence—as a practitioner—on your co-workers rather than on the nameless thousands your organisation sets out to assist.

Apprentice: Sometimes I wish we could go back to an older time when life was simpler and you lived with your tribe on the land.

Teachers: It is impractical to get too romantic about ancient cultures. They were made up of human beings just as ours is. Although they may have lived more harmoniously with the land and the seasons—from necessity—they still would have engaged in the same patterns of dualistic derangement in which modern-day human beings indulge.

Bad-mouthing

Apprentice: In my job I have trouble dealing with one of my colleagues. She is very dominant and speaks badly about other people. She even speaks ill of some of our clients. I find it hard to accept this behaviour.

Teachers: It may be that speaking badly about other people and your clients is a coping strategy for her, and that she does not mean what she says very seriously. It may be that she is someone who needs to vocalise as a release valve. Even if this is not in fact the case, it might help you to feel more kindly towards her if you view it in this way.

People have different methods of coping with the situations they come across in life – some people express their emotions while others suppress them, and then others dissipate them through activity. It sounds as though she is someone who is expressive—more expressive than is comfortable for you—but this does not mean that she would necessarily follow through on her comments. As she is in a caring profession it is reasonable to assume that she cares about others. You cannot account for the behaviour of others – you can only be responsible for your own. Aim to be the best example of the behaviour you'd like to see.

Apprentice: I try to see her positive aspects but unfortunately this doesn't last long and then I find myself back to rejecting her behaviour.

Teachers: Every time you focus on her positive aspects feel happy that you have tried. Every time you try is a success – even if your dislike of her behaviour arises again. If you interact with her in terms of her positive qualities and ignore the aspects of her personality that you find difficult, you may find that you can develop a useful working relationship.

5

Sangha

In the Aro gTér Tradition, a teacher's sangha consists of their apprentices. There is the wider sangha of Aro gTér practitioners, the even wider sangha of Nyingma practitioners, and an ever widening circle of Tibetan Buddhists and Buddhists of all schools – but a teacher's immediate body of apprentices is their sangha. Ngakma Nor'dzin and Ngakpa 'ö-Dzin place a strong emphasis on the role of sangha in their teachings.

Most practitioners will be aware of the four-fold refuge prevalent in Tibetan Buddhism: Lama, Buddha, Dharma, Sangha.[1] Without going into a detailed discussion of the meaning of refuge,[2] what is worthy of note here is that sangha —the community of practitioners—is considered as important a source of refuge as is the Lama, the Buddha and the teachings themselves. This is because in Vajrayana a certain 'chemistry' between the teacher and their students needs to exist in order for transmission and authentic practice to be possible. This chemistry can only take place if the conditions in the 'laboratory' are right. These conditions are called the five certainties: the certain teacher, the certain teaching, the certain time, the certain place and the certain retinue (or sangha).

---

1   In Tibetan: Lama (bLa ma), Sang-gyé (sang rGyas), Chö (chos) and Gendün (dGe 'gun). The fourfold refuge is particular to Tibetan Buddhism, the more common form of refuge is threefold: Buddha, Dharma and Sangha.
2   Tibetan kyab (sKyabs)

When one of these certainties is missing, transmission cannot occur. Sangha, as a 'certainty', means that the students around the teacher play a role in creating the right environment for the teaching to be authentically given, and authentically received. The atmosphere of the sangha is of critical importance: students must practise seeing the teacher and each other with pure view. It is often said that if interpersonal difficulties exist between just two members of a sangha, then the opportunity for transmission is lost to all the other practitioners.

Fostering such an environment is a theme to which Ngakma Nor'dzin and Ngakpa 'ö-Dzin often return. A sangha where students attempt to see each other with pure view has a remarkable effect in that it encourages greater openness and a sense of spacious appreciation. The Buddhist view is that we are all beginninglessly enlightened, and so having one's fellow students reflect this by holding us in pure view can dramatically facilitate our capacity to see ourselves as enlightened beings. This ambiance is what allows students to release their self-protectiveness and take risks at being more genuine human beings. Sangha is the safe environment where we can experiment, before taking the practice out into the wider world.

Practising with sangha in this way is not always easy. Our fellow sangha members start to become 'annoying friends' in that they cease to support our neuroses. They no longer support us in indulging our tendencies towards cliquishness, and do not join us in criticising others. Their example pushes us in the direction of kindness and openness.

Editor

Pure view

Apprentice: Thanks again for being there for me. It is a tremendous boost to my practice. Gradually coming to feel more and more part of a sangha is also incredibly supportive. How is interaction with the sangha connected with pure view?

Teachers: To belong to a sangha and to be able to immerse oneself in the pure view of a practising Vajrayana community is an extraordinary opportunity. You can let go of self image and posturing; you can let go of needing to impress others or wishing to appear in a good light; you can let go of needing to be liked and appreciated, because being liked and appreciated is the ground of vajra sangha; you can let go of the fear of others' limited views and misconceptions about you, because trust is the ground of the vajra sangha; you can let go of needing company and fearing isolation. You can free-flow in awareness-presence and discover the liberation of that experience.

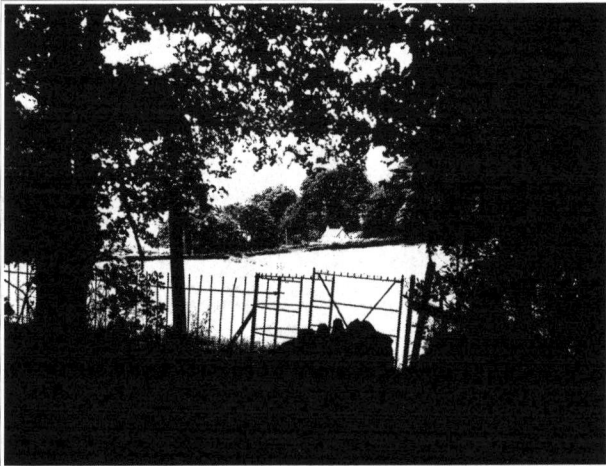

The Annoying Friend

Apprentice: A question came into my mind, which I've already had for some time, concerning talking and listening to each other as apprentices. It's well understood that unsolicited advice is inappropriate, but I wonder how to react when another apprentice is talking about their failures or running down their qualities. I find this quite difficult, because it's not inspiring for them or for me either, when I just listen or when I contradict.

Teachers: Anything they say about their own qualities, whether they think they're good or bad, is self-referential, and their own view of themselves is always suspect. Whether they're praising themselves or running themselves down, there's some kind of pay-off, even if it is the familiarity of their own misery, or an escape from the apparent effort of simply being who they are. Perhaps if they say negative things about themselves their ordinary friends continually deny this and assure them that they are fine. Perhaps they find this comforting and allow a pattern to be created of expressing self-deprecation in order to again be comforted.

Sangha members are the annoying friends who help each other to be real in the world and live their lives as practitioners. They do not offer the comforting platitudes, but they also have to be careful with their directness. Sangha members do not want to add to the person's negative view of themselves by confronting them with the cause of discomfort.

Dwelling on shortcomings gets in the way of developing pure view. It makes it more difficult for others to view them as a realised being, and it makes it difficult for them to view themselves as beginninglessly enlightened. Remember that their miserable expression of their view of themselves is directly linked with their enlightened nature: their avarice with generosity, their anger with clarity, and even their depression with intelligence. If you can see this then a helpful response might suggest itself.

Being shy

New apprentice: Usually I am quiet and a bit reserved. I feel this may be a hindrance as an apprentice. Can you offer some advice on this?

Teachers: There is nothing particularly problematic with being quiet and reserved – in fact this is preferable to being brash and insensitive. It demonstrates a capacity for self-restraint. You may find you gradually feel less reserved as you gain more experience of engaging with sangha. One of the purposes of the sangha—the vajra family—is that it provides an arena in which trust can be developed. The vajra family are a group of people who are actively attempting to develop and hold pure view. On retreat the vajra family especially attempts to maintain pure view of their vajra brothers and sisters. They assume that their vajra brothers and sisters are also engaging with this practice.

This means that you can trust that your fellow retreatants welcome interaction with you, and that they are interested in what you have to say and will respond kindly. If you say something clumsy or inappropriate you trust that they will not ridicule you, but will wish to help you to communicate more effectively. If you hear a vajra sibling speaking in a way that seems hurtful or unkind, you entertain the possibility that they didn't mean it like that and respond in a kind and open manner.

Apprenticeship provides an arena where you can take a risk in relative safety. It is acting from a perspective of openness and kindness with the conviction that this is what the rest of your sangha are also attempting to do.

You practice this with your vajra family where relative safety is assured, in preparation for engaging with pure view in the larger sphere of everyday life where safety is absolutely not guaranteed.

Reservation and quietness are reasonable coping strategies for ordinary life. However within the context of the vajra family you are correct in thinking that they could become drawbacks to transmission and inspiration. Ultimately all coping strategies become barriers to realisation, but to begin with it would be foolish to simply drop them all. You will find that as practice develops and your capacity for kindness and awareness grows, you will start to let go of your coping strategies.

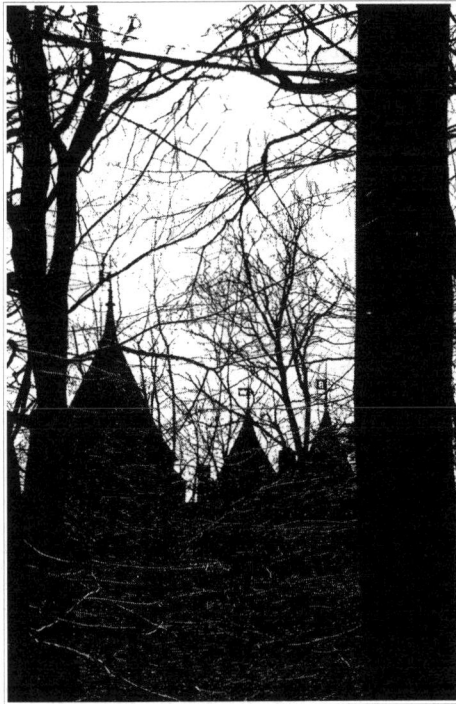

Working hard

Apprentice: I am starting to see this pattern of me 'doing my own thing'. I think it is that the focus of my attention on my own activities leads sometimes to a lack of awareness of the whole picture of what is happening and my place in that as part of a vajra family. I can understand this – but to be able to see and realise it in the moment is quite a different matter altogether.

Teachers: Seeing it and understanding it in retrospect is the springboard for diving into the awareness of it in the moment. Keep bringing yourself back to awareness of when it has occurred or is occurring. Gradually your capacity to be aware of it and let it go in the moment will increase.

Apprentice: I fear inactivity and emptiness, especially when I can see something can be done that I am capable of doing.

Teachers: On a retreat it is always good to have apprentices who have plenty of energy and who are aware of things that need doing. We appreciate this capacity. However the tension that arose around this on the retreat was that you continually reproached others and did not seem to find it easy to work with them and be part of a team. At face value working hard in the kitchen whilst others are sitting around, would appear to be noble. However if you are building up irritation and resentment while working – this is not skilful. If work needs to be done and you have noticed it and others have not, then it is possible and reasonable to ask for help in an open-hearted and friendly manner.

Apprentice: How am I to go about working with this in terms of transformation without slipping into a form of neurotic inertia where confidence disappears?

Teachers: Being the person who does everything but never sits in the garden with their vajra siblings during quiet periods has become an evasion – a means of maintaining a view of yourself that is comfortable and familiar. For you sitting with your vajra family chatting and simply being natural is the challenging aspect of retreats. This is where you feel vulnerable and where you find it difficult to trust that you are liked and valued as part of the vajra family.

Being busy in the kitchen is easier for you and less threatening – but then you feel taken for granted and start to feel resentful … which makes your behaviour less open and friendly … so you become less approachable for the others and more isolated. It is a self-maintaining cycle. This is samsara.

Everyone has some cyclic pattern of this sort—or many—so you are lucky to have spotted a primary one for you. There is no simple answer for overcoming this, other than practice. Practise shi-nè and your patterns will gradually become transparent. It is true that it would be as neurotic to simply stop being a busy, helpful person when on retreat. Simply try to be aware of when being busy is actually a strategy to avoiding being social, and notice when resentment bubbles up.

6

The Hell of Being a Practitioner

Buddhist practice develops kindness and awareness in ourselves, but the path of practice can be a bumpy one – to say the least. As we discover qualities of openness and appreciation, we are also confronted with what we have always been, but have chosen to ignore. We begin to see our territoriality, our aggressiveness, our neediness, our jealousy and our obduracy. We become aware of the sides of ourselves that we find distinctly less 'spiritual'.

When we practise silent sitting—shi-nè—we get acquainted with ourselves. We begin to face our own minds and progressively discover our psychological make-up. Once the mental chatter that distracts us from the directness of practice starts to subside, we are left with the uncomfortable discovery of our neurotic patterning.

Relationship with the teacher will turn the heat up. Because the teacher sees us as we really are and recognises the enlightened potential of our neurotic tendencies, they act as a mirror for the student. The teacher allows the student to catch glimpses of their realised qualities, but also puts a magnifying glass on the neurotic tendencies.

This can be a hellish experience as we struggle to present those aspects of ourselves we believe to be worthy, and try to hide what we believe is less presentable. The teacher will play with this till we begin to realise that what we see as our neurotic side is actually also our realised nature.

When we learn to relax, struggle ceases, and those many insurmountable problems we had turn out to be irrelevant. I would imagine that, from the teacher's point of view, our struggles must be both tragic and highly amusing in that struggle is what causes the problem in the first place.

The hell of being a practitioner is a series of dialogues where students present their own struggles, their own 'mini hells' of neurosis, vulnerability, frustration, doubt, or lack of commitment. These hells are especially hellish when we have come to realise that they are maintained because of our tendency to struggle – yet we find ourselves unable to relinquish the struggle.

Editor

Storm mind

Apprentice: I thought I could get over my upset with some kind of willpower, which I obviously cannot. I know that the states of mind I am working myself into are not going to disappear miraculously.

Teachers: States of mind arise and dissolve. Any state of mind will move and change and eventually dissolve – especially if you avoid 'working yourself into' it.

Apprentice: I have knowledge enough to know that relaxing is the way out of the hell-realm, but the storm in my mind seems to be running on autopilot.

Teachers: Storms can be frightening – but they can also be exciting and exhilarating if you can have the confidence to ride them. There is a lot of energy in a storm. The mind cannot be controlled and forced to behave. The mind will do what it does based on your individual patterning. The more you try to force a pattern out of the mind, the more prominence it will have in your life. Similarly you will not succeed in forcing a pattern into the mind even if it would seem preferable to your existing mind-state.

Intensity

Apprentice: My practice seems to be bringing up a lot of insecurity and fear these days. It started when I began practising more intensely.

There's been a lot of 'staring into emotions', which has been instructive, but it hasn't been a very pleasant time.

Teachers: When you start to practise more intensely all sorts of aspects of yourself suddenly seem to come into focus and insist you notice them. These have always been there, but safely tucked away where you could previously ignore them. This is what Ngakpa 'ö-Dzin calls 'the hell of being a practitioner'. Practice —especially Vajrayana—is like grabbing the bare electricity cables and inviting the shock. If the intensity is becoming too much, then ease off a little for a while. Engage in simple practice such as shi-nè, and inspirational practice such as Lama'i Naljor and yogic song.[1] Physical practice may help as well. Perhaps have a few short practice sessions rather than one long one. When you feel a little more settled again you can increase the intensity once more. Remember, this is a marathon, not a sprint and you have to learn to pace yourself – knowing when to ease off and when to push through. It sounds as though this may be a time to ease off for a while.

---

1   Lama'i Naljor (*bLa ma'i rNal 'byor*) is the practice of unifying with the mind of the Lama. Yogic song—Dzogchen gar-dang (*rDzogs chen sGar gDangs*)—is the practice of finding presence of awareness in the dimension of sound.

The lonely path

Apprentice: Sometimes I feel that being a practitioner is quite a lonely path.

Teachers: A practitioner is alone—in terms of being a practitioner —if they are surrounded by non-practitioners. But there are many situations where this could apply. A rugby player may feel alone if surrounded by golfers; a wine drinker may feel alone if surrounded by beer drinkers. In some sense you are all always alone and yet you are also always surrounded by beings. If you choose to dwell on being alone then this can become a problem. Indulging in emptiness can be as unhelpful as indulging in form. There will always be something you are getting out of it – some pay off in terms of referentiality that makes your indulgence worthwhile. Find out what you are getting out of dwelling on the loneliness of being a practitioner and then you may be able to let this habit dissolve.

Faking

Apprentice: During the recent retreat I had the feeling that I was faking practice. I felt cut off from everything.

Teachers: It isn't really possible to 'fake' silent sitting. It is so direct that it simply is as it is. We suppose it is possible to 'fake' enjoying the company of your sangha, the teachings and being with us.

Feeling cut off could be a coping strategy, a means of protecting oneself from the deliciously dangerous nakedness of being that can be experienced on an apprentice retreat. Being viewed as a dakini and viewing others as dakas and dakinis [2] is courageous and challenging – and hence not always comfortable.

2   Viewing and being viewed as a Dakini or Daka (khandro, *'mKha' 'gro*, and pawo, *dPa' bo*, in Tibetan) relates to the practice of pure view. One practises seeing vajra sisters and brothers as enlightened beings.

Owning our emotions

Apprentice: My partner is out of hospital now. He has had good care, but has found the whole experience frightening and miserable, and it has left him feeling vulnerable.

Teachers: Yes, we can imagine that it has.

Apprentice: I am trying my best to be kind in the way he wants to be supported, though I have been finding this quite difficult. I want to do things for him and he wants to do everything for himself. He has been quite unpleasant at times.

Teachers: Nursing people can be quite a challenge. You may have to forgive him if he is more grumpy and difficult than usual. However this should be tempered with your right to be treated decently as well.

Illness, tiredness, grief, stress, pain, old age—the list could be endless—are not valid reasons to justify unpleasant behaviour towards other people. Practitioners try to avoid the self-indulgence of emotion. You could gently point this out to him if his behaviour becomes really unreasonable. It is important to own emotional states whatever life circumstances are being experienced.

Flirting

Apprentice: I've just started to realise that I'm a dreadful flirt!

Teachers: It's important to understand that these things you notice about yourself have always been there – you just start to see it because of practice. You are not suddenly becoming a more neurotic person or developing new bad habits. Playfulness in relationship with others is fine as long as it does not undermine or conflict with your relationship with your partner, or the flirting becomes inappropriately sexual in its nature. If the flirting overflows into fantasising about another person or wishing for a romantic relationship with someone other than your partner, then there is the danger of this becoming adulterous. If it becomes behaviour that suggests inappropriate intent, then this is not conducive to whole-hearted conduct. Playfulness is enjoyable for everyone, but must include awareness, and honourable behaviour and intent.

Safety

Apprentice: My life is so time-consuming and absorbing that I act in a laissez-faire attitude towards apprenticeship. But please prod away and I'll do my best to either pass or fail with dignity.

Teachers: Life will always be time-consuming. It is a matter of being realistic about one's aspirations and priorities. If practice and apprenticeship are important to you, then you will find time for them. If you continually fail to find time for them then perhaps you need to examine how important they are for you.

Apprentice: I am working with my neuroses every day especially paranoia, the air element. It's outrageous how it just springs out at me – enemies and persecutors and possible pitfalls everywhere. But in this very moment I am safe – or am I? What do I think? If a moment is no time then I guess there's room for safety in that, safety in the naked moment?

Teachers: There is only 'the safety of no safety'. There is the safety of each moment being exactly as it is – so yes, 'the naked moment' is an apt phrase. A lack of safety is created by clinging to an expectation of what the moment will be. Lack of safety is experienced when it becomes apparent that reality will differ from expectation. Feeling unsafe arises when reality threatens your illusion.

Arising emotion

Apprentice: Practice seems to be bringing to the surface particular emotional energies. I am very aware of a lot of feelings of resentment, frustration and anger arising in practice at the moment. Why is this?

Teachers: It is generally not worth intellectualising too much about 'why' something is. Such 'why' questions do not generally go anywhere. It is as it is. Just observe how you are and let it go. This emotion has always been there but you have not been aware of it. When you start to allow the mind to settle through practice, all sorts of things may manifest.

Apprentice: I have been spending more time than previously in my silent sitting as I am sure this helps with letting go of the concepts when I am having a powerful emotional experience. I am sure that I have quite a lot of repressed emotions—especially anger—and releasing these and learning to work or play creatively with them has been an ongoing theme for me.

Teachers: It is pretty much an on-going theme for everyone. If you are experiencing a great deal of powerful emotion you may also find it helpful to engage in yogic song. This can allow the energy to transform. Also you could try to observe where you feel the emotion in your body and focus on the sensation. The important thing is to not get involved in the intellectual concept around the energetic emotion.

Being a practitioner

Apprentice: It has been a difficult period of doubt, but yes, I now know that I cannot actually stop being a practitioner any more... fortunately!

Teachers: It is wonderful to hear you say this. This makes everything possible. It also makes everything simple. Once you know at a fundamental level of your being that you *are* a practitioner and nothing will ever change that ... eventual success in practice is guaranteed. You're on the path – which is indistinguishable from the goal.

Meaningless

Apprentice: All practices seem somehow meaningless in my current state of mind.

Teachers: Practice is as meaningful as eating. You eat your breakfast, lunch and dinner today, and then you have to eat again tomorrow … and the next day … and the next … Every day the same. It is meaningful in that it sustains you but meaningless in that as soon as the occupation is complete you are moving towards needing to do it again.

Practitioners practise. It is what they do. Sometimes it may feel that there is no point in sitting today, and then again tomorrow, and the next day … and the next … It is meaningful even when it feels meaningless because it sustains you as a practitioner.

Maybe you could stop practising for a while and see what happens. If you no longer practise then what? Perhaps it would be interesting to find out.

Apprentice: I feel that I have let you down.

Teachers: We always remain open to being delighted – but generally we do not attach to ideas about people that may lead to disappointment. You are who you are and your patterning is acute sometimes and less so at other times. Doubt will always arise occasionally. It does not mean that you have to give everything up and react in an extreme manner. Everything is workable – this is the nature of Vajrayana, but that is if you want it to be workable.

When a practitioner experiences doubt they sit anyway and see what happens. When things feel meaningless they sit anyway and sit with the pointlessness. Practice is life, life is practice. That is all there is. Practice can be formal or informal, organised or chaotic, intense or relaxed. For tantrikas life is practice.

The path is the goal

Apprentice: I have two extremes of feeling really inspired and motivated and then feeling I'm not sure why I'm doing this – or maybe it's more a case of 'Can I do this?'

Teachers: This is common experience – oscillating between inspired motivation uncertainty. Enjoy the times of inspired motivation and the energy this generates. When you feel unsure as to why you are practising, allow the thread of confidence in your practice, and your relationship with us, to keep you at it. This is where effort and self-discipline come into play.

With regard to 'Can I do this?' in a sense the answer is 'No' – because it is the *needing to do it* that means you cannot. As soon as you can do it, you won't need to do it any more. The path is the goal. Once you have arrived at the goal you no longer need to travel the path. Once you are travelling the path you are discovering the goal.

Apprentice: I guess to a large extent my swinging feelings come from me expecting something definite to happen to indicate that I'm 'getting somewhere'.

Teachers: The signs of 'getting somewhere' may be quite subtle and unexpected. Holding to a particular idea of 'getting somewhere' may distort your experience by yearning and hunting, so that you miss the actual signs of 'getting somewhere'. You are as you are and if you continue to practice – 'getting somewhere' is guaranteed.

Distraction

Apprentice: It's easier to get hurt and angry and distant than to sit with and stare into my pain.

Teachers: Of course it is. This is what you have always done in the past. You are used to being reactive and it takes time to be able to simply sit with the sensation you are experiencing. Being a practitioner is not easy. Being a practitioner is damned inconvenient – because you can no longer indulge the patterns that have become transparent through practice.

Apprentice: If I am on my own a lot, such as when my partner is away, I can feel really thrown – as if there is so much space around me that I didn't know what to do. So I eat, drink, watch TV, pace the house in a crazed manner. It actually frightens me to sit still, so I haven't been practising.

Teachers: In terms of practice, if sitting still is too much to cope with—so that shi-nè is not possible—practise yogic song instead. There is more energy and form in this practice and it will help you face your aversion to the emptiness you are experiencing. sKu-mNyé would also be good. If at other times you feel that you need to distract yourself from emptiness, going for a walk or listening to music will be more worthwhile than numbing the mind with television, alcohol and too much food. Keep the sense fields open and enjoy the infinite array of sensual delights available to you.

Justification

Apprentice: I'm still not quite sure I understand what you mean about anger and self-justifying it.

Teachers: Well perhaps the best way to illustrate this would be to use an example. Earlier someone came into the shrine room a little late and said: *'I'm sorry I'm late – but nobody told me what time we were starting.'* A statement such as this displays irritation and a sense of having a right to be irritated. It is saying: *'I am late because you didn't tell me what time I should have been here and so it is your fault.'* It may make all those within earshot feel that they are being reproached. There was no sense of taking responsibility in this statement – either for being late for the session or for the irritation that created the need to tell everyone that they believed it was their fault.

It can never be assumed that it is anyone else's fault that you missed out on learning the starting time of the next session; or that you failed to hear the announcement that tea was being enjoyed in the living room; or that you can't find your notebook. Everyone has lapses of concentration. Most people wander off at times so that they are not in the right place at the right time to hear the announcement. Everyone misplaces things.

Let's look at the situation from the perspective suggested in the statement. Why would their sangha exclude them from knowing the time of the session? Do they believe they are nasty people who are actively scheming to make them late? Have the sangha gathered together and decided as a group that they are not going to tell them the time of the session?

Did they know that this individual was ignorant of the session starting time and wilfully withhold the information? It starts to look silly when you analyse the accusation implicit in the justification of their irritation.

On retreat practitioners hold one another in pure view. They always assume that the sangha has their best interests at heart and that they will never knowingly treat them thoughtlessly, overlook them, or mess with their possessions. In return they do the same for their vajra brothers and sisters – they look out for them and treat them with consideration and respect. The mind that views others in this way is free of irritation and the need to reproach anyone. The situation remains open with genuine, open-hearted regret for being late without any stickiness of guilt or blame. *'I'm sorry I'm late'* would have been quite sufficient.

And so it begins

New Apprentice: When we first met I was very inspired and still am, however I have a tendency to be a good starter and poor finisher – or should I say fast starter and slow thereafter. It's the same when I'm drinking wine!

Teachers: If there is still inspiration we do not see any problem in going slowly. Apprenticeship is a marathon not a sprint. We would stress the importance of practising every day, but there is no particular need for practice to become an intense experience. Gradual progress through regular practice is more sustainable than intense bursts of practice.

New Apprentice: My passion hasn't gone cold but I'm afraid to let others down – so perhaps in fact I simply let myself down.

Teachers: You will not let us down by being confused or uncertain.

New Apprentice: Perhaps the best I can do at the moment is to hang in there with my apprenticeship and see how it goes. I don't know why I worry about being a burden or feel pressure of expectation – this sense is totally self-induced. Yourselves and the sangha have given nothing but love and support, allowing me total freedom to indulge in my neurosis.

Teachers: It is useful to notice habit patterns and also a sign of the benefit of practice. We are glad that you have felt warmly received by ourselves and the sangha. Hopefully this environment of practitioners will also give you total freedom to let go of your neurosis.

New Apprentice: Perhaps reaching a point at which I was thinking of leaving apprenticeship has become the point at which I can really start with my apprenticeship – like facing the worst that could happen and working from there. I find a strange security in that. Now any small progress I can make feels like an achievement.

Teachers: This is how it goes sometimes. You discover that what you believe to be a terrible thing, is not actually so bad, and that your teachers aren't actually shocked or horrified at what you tell them. We will never judge you or condemn you, but only attempt to help you view your situation and patterning through Dharma so that everything is available for spontaneous liberation.

Heroism

Apprentice: I have been feeling quite desperate and wanted to be near you somehow, but then thought that I cannot run to you when life gets a bit rough – I should be grown up.

Teachers: Yes it is true that you have to be adult and cope with your problems – but you do not always have to be tough with yourself. It is fine to seek comfort sometimes and we are happy to hear that being with us represents some comfort for you. Life has been exceedingly rough for you recently and you are coping well.

Apprentice: I am thankful that I can email or telephone with you for some help and advice.

Teachers: We have been impressed with the manner in which you have kept in touch through these difficulties – asking sensible questions and expressing the pain you are feeling clearly, without self-pity. You have been prepared to approach the situation as a practitioner, have listened to our suggestions and acted upon them. This is not so common.

Apprentice: I have not always behaved like a hero in the last few weeks. I was really desperate and I still am sometimes.

Teachers: We have to disagree – you have approached the situation as a practitioner and that is in itself heroic. It is extraordinary. You have felt regretful when resentment has arisen. You have tried to remain open-hearted – this is the quality of heroism. You have not always succeeded but you have always tried.

You have recognised when anger and other unhelpful emotions have crept up on you and tried to transform them. It will take time for this turmoil to subside – but it will subside.

When strong emotion arises, see that it is like a wave that swells and then breaks. Have confidence that the dissolving of emotions is as certain as their arising. This will help you to be less at the mercy of the emotions and avoid saying or doing things that you may later regret. Try to ride the wave rather than being swept along with it, thrashing about in the spume. Remember the three possible approaches [3] to engaging with the emotion and continue to do your best.

Apprentice: I sometimes find it difficult to keep a practitioner's point of view and to remain open. It is all so overwhelmingly painful.

Teachers: It is of course overwhelmingly painful – but your desire to maintain the view of a practitioner even in this difficult situation is something to celebrate. It will get easier and you will eventually come out the other side knowing that you have acted honourably and with dignity. Being a practitioner does not make pain go away, but you will be able to look back at this time eventually and recognise that you are a hero.

---

3   'Three possible approaches' refers to the methods of Sutra, Tantra and Dzogchen: renunciation, transformation and spontaneous realisation.

Does samsara really exist?

Apprentice: I've been feeling the need to have more sense of spaciousness. I sometimes have tried to plunge into lengthier practices every day, but often I can't sustain it for more than a couple of weeks or so, and then I just feel frustrated at not keeping it up. So this time what I'm trying to do is to include more unplanned short sits throughout the day (and night sometimes). If I have a five or ten spare minutes, or if I feel the need, I just stop and sit wherever I am … this is really helping.

Teachers: Excellent. This is very good – finding your own way into practice and adapting and adjusting to find out what works for you. This is a useful way to really ease into the discovery that every moment is practice. Enjoy the times when you are able to practise more, but relax with the times when you cannot practise so much. Always maintain the thread of being a practitioner. As you become more experienced as a practitioner, you will find that it will be beneficial to have longer meditation sessions at some point.

Apprentice: One confusion I have at the moment is does samsara actually exist? There are moments when I'm not entirely sure right now. It's as if I could let go of seeing things as good or bad in the ordinary way completely. Then I worry if this wouldn't be to abandon common sense. How would I deal with harmful situations or day-to-day conflicts if everything is simply the Natural State? [4]

---

4 The natural state is the enlightened condition of the individual. The term is connected to Dzogchen where duality is considered a mere distortion of our fundamental nature.

Teachers: Samsara exists because of duality. It can easily cease to exist in the moment through changing your view. Dwelling in the natural state would not mean that you lack the ability to act – your actions would be totally appropriate and compassionate. It is possible to be wrathful without being angry. It is possible to be destructive where the situation requires it without this being out-of-control energy. It is possible to make a stand without justification and self-protective posturing. To dwell in the natural state would be to be a Dharma warrior.

Conceptual rehearsal

Apprentice: Recent horrors on the news have left me feeling frightened about my family. Our lives seem so tenuous and there seem to be so many ways to die. My daughter is abroad at the moment and I worry that something might happen to her and I will never see her again. This is making me feel really miserable.

Teachers: You are correct that life is tenuous – you may die before you have read this, and so may we. Terrible things do happen in the world and there is the possibility of losing loved ones.

It does not change the situation however, to dwell on this, and it does not help anyone to become miserable with worry. Imagining terrible things does not prepare you for when bad things do happen or prevent them from actually happening. It is common to daydream about the horrors-that-might-be. This can be a way of attempting to keep them at bay. You think that if you are able to conjure an image of the worst thing that could happen to you, then it probably won't happen. You feel that if you have lived through it in your mind, it probably will not happen and if—heaven forbid—it does happen, at least you are prepared. It is a coping strategy.

The reality of what actually happens in your life will simply be as it is. It will not be like your conceptual rehearsal. Whatever happens will happen. The only useful way to prepare yourself for unfortunate circumstances is to practise being aware and present in every moment.

The problems of the world touch you more or less at different times in your life. If you allow the suffering and disasters of the world to become the causes for despondency and despair, you are not helping anyone – in fact you are adding to the world's problems.

Apprentice: When I read about these terrible things I start to wonder what is the point of meditating and reciting mantra. How can this help to solve the real problems in the world? It seems rather self-centred.

Teachers: Your practice of shi-nè and mantra is not going to miraculously manifest food in the mouths of the starving, or a roof over the heads of the homeless. However your practice makes you different, and this difference can have an influence on everybody and everything you touch. Your practice creates a little prism that facilitates the sparkling through of realisation. It can feel as though this is centred on yourself when you practise alone a lot of the time, but as your practice changes how you respond to people and situations, that prism can radiate to a surprising degree. Being—or attempting to be—a present, aware and honourable human being affects all who come into contact with you. Having a kind and friendly approach to life influences your circumstances. If every human being was kind and honourable, many of the problems in the world would mysteriously dissolve – but there would still be the chaotic dance of events being exactly as they are.

Secondary causes

Apprentice: I feel ashamed of the story I told you about how I got my own back on my landlady. I keep going over it and feel more and more miserable and guilty about it.

Teachers: The story you told us about your interaction with your landlady was not a happy one – but you did recognise that you reacted from the need for revenge and retribution and have regretted this. You recognised that your aggression produced feelings of insecurity and worry – rather than courage and a feeling of being in control that you might have expected from a conventional perspective.

You have had a stressful time recently and your landlady has not been sympathetic or helpful. This does not excuse unskilful actions, but it does offer an explanation. You have to rip out the heart of self-justification, but you also have to recognise the error and not protract it conceptually when you get it wrong. Each moment is a new moment. That situation and reaction is in the past. It cannot be changed, but it has been regretted. You must now look forward to how you can avoid getting into that type of situation with your landlady again, and live with the intention of been impeccably honourable and direct in your dealings with her from here on.

Apprentice: Is my landlady a secondary cause?

Teachers: Yes indeed. External factors spark patterns of perception you do not know you have.

Life is a little like walking through a minefield – you never know when you may step on something—a circumstance of your life —that will explode a programmed pattern of perception. If the cause is not encountered the reaction will not occur. One of the principles of the monastic path is to regulate the secondary causes—in terms of life circumstances—as much as possible to avoid triggering unhelpful reactions that deepen patterning. The tantric path however says: 'Bring it all on!' so that you have the opportunity to transform distorted perception and response into enlightened perception and response.

Why am I here?

Apprentice: A couple of weeks ago I felt like being an apprentice was a real inconvenience and that it was annoying me.

Teachers: It is inevitable that times will arise when practice and being part of a lineage will feel like an inconvenience. The lineage is larger than you and hence sometimes makes demands that do not fit in with your personal plans.

Apprentice: I thought how lovely it would be to pack it all in and forget about effortless effort.

Teachers: Your use of this term suggests that awareness is arising and understanding is deepening through your practice, so perhaps it would be a shame to stop?

Apprentice: Then I thought about how unpleasant it would be to give it up – how it would feel like a missed opportunity. I thought about how much I enjoy being part of this tradition and how special it all is.

Teachers: We are happy to hear that you feel this way.

Apprentice: Then I thought, but why do I want to be part of it all and realised that I didn't really know. Why is it? I guess I see it as a chance to feel happy and good and safe and part of a family on an adventure. There are also thoughts of enlightenment and Buddhas and the end of suffering and being more peaceful or more alive.

Teachers: Is it important to know? Is not-knowing part of the adventure? Feeling happy will certainly increase if you practise, as will feeling more alive.

You may also become a kinder person and so feel good about that and more peaceful. Conventional safety is not guaranteed through practice, although the capacity to feel comfortable with a lack of safety may increase. 'Enlightenment', 'Buddhas' and 'the end of suffering' we would suggest are too grand and unfathomable to be reasons to keep one's practice continuing on a day-by-day basis, but they function as aspiration and inspiration.

Apprentice: Then I came back to thinking that I still don't know really why I am part of the lineage, and how strange, special, inconvenient and time-consuming it all is when I could be doing other stuff. It all just seemed to go round and round in circles.

Teachers: Yes you could be doing 'other stuff' – and that would also be fine. It is not really what you do that is important, but more how you do it. This is the teaching of the Mahasiddhas. However in order to affect the how-you-do-stuff you need to have awareness, and in order to have awareness you have to engage in a method that enables you to discover awareness … and so you return to the need to practise. It is good to experience and admit to such times of uncertainty. It is not realistic to expect to always feel totally sure and involved. If you practise you will change and perhaps you will enjoy those changes. You may notice others who are practising change, and be inspired by those changes and the kindness and insight you see arising spontaneously. Experience creates certainty and confidence that could manifest as awareness and kindness.

Manipulation

Apprentice: How can I find out what is the purpose of my life? Sometimes it feels so hollow and pointless even though I practise. I feel as though I am manipulating my reality.

Teachers: There is no purpose to life—in the sense of an ultimate purpose—there is only purpose in the moment. To give a simple example: there is a purpose in brushing your teeth because it will make your mouth feel nicer and help prevent gum disease so that your teeth don't fall out. Your life will be more comfortable with a mouth full of teeth in healthy gums. However eventually your gums will rot and your teeth fall out—if not while you are alive, then certainly after you are dead—so there is no ultimate purpose in brushing your teeth. Being aware of the transient, in-the-moment purpose of brushing teeth, you do so conscientiously, beautifully, with presence of mind – brushing teeth becomes an art form. It has its own purpose.

Apprentice: Isn't finding meaning in the moment manipulative – creating something that isn't there? Isn't practice merely a different sort of manipulation?

Teachers: Practice could be seen as skilful manipulation. The aim of practice is to become kind and happy people, who benefit others and avoid harm. Practice skilfully manipulates your dualistic condition to change it into the realised state. You are not attempting to change a situation to a predetermined state, you are trying to open the situation and encourage clarity so that it can be exactly what it is. The outcome is open and undefined.

Apprentice: I feel as though I am battling with the reality of my situation.

Teachers: You may be experiencing a sense of battling because you are not allowing the situation to open *of itself*, but are trying to force something to happen. If your experience is a lack of purpose, then that is the experience of that moment and you enter the dimension of purposelessness. We would advise that you do not try to force a sense of purpose into it.

Regret

Apprentice: I bumped into an old acquaintance from my drug-taking days – and the inevitable happened and I ended up getting high. This then was the beginning of a cycle of guilt and relapse into drug taking.[5] Eventually I asserted my self-control and stopped taking everything, and have been drug free since then. So this is why I have not been in touch for quite a long time – I was waiting until I could present myself again in a respectable manner.

Teachers: The relationship with the teacher does not demand that we only see our apprentices 'at their best.' There is absolutely no need to 'put a brave face on things' and try to assure us everything is going fine when it isn't. We may even start to be a little suspicious if this is the only face we ever see. It is the warts and barnacles of your being that are your practice – so please feel free to present yourself in whatever form you are manifesting.

All we ask is that you are open and honest, polite and friendly. We may have been able to help you through this period of relapse, and support you while extricating yourself from the reassertion of your involvement with drugs. If this happens again, please do get in touch at the time rather than waiting until you have sorted yourself out.

Apprentice: I had wanted to contact you from the very first time I relapsed – however I felt too ashamed.

---

5   The taking of drugs is not permitted within the context of apprenticeship in the Aro gTér sanghas. Drugs, like tobacco, damage the subtle energetic body and prevent genuine progress in practice.

Teachers: Everyone relapses into neurotic patterning all the time. This pattern is no more harmful than any other neurotic pattern – in fact less harmful than many in that it is only hurting you and not others. Regret is useful, but shame simply adds another layer of neurosis to plough through. Regret the relapse and move on. Shame is actually holding on to it and not allowing yourself to move on. Regret the action and let it go – this is simple, clean and straightforward.

7

Practice and Openness

A recurring theme in Ngakma Nor'dzin and Ngakpa 'ö-Dzin's teachings is the encouragement to develop a greater sense of openness. The word 'openness' can tend to be used as a synonym for 'awareness', but whereas awareness can be understood in a wide variety of ways, 'openness' is somewhat more straightforward. Ngakpa 'ö-Dzin describes it as the 'capacity to remain uncertain about the outcome of a given situation'.

Openness is the key to Tantra in that it allows us to start relinquishing our tight grip on our definitions and preconceptions about how things should be. When I can remain open about a situation, and consider various outcomes without necessarily being fixed on the one I prefer, I begin to entertain the capacity for ambivalence.

Ambivalence is the experience of having simultaneous conflicting feelings about a situation – being attracted to something and simultaneously put off. Most of the time, ambivalent situations make us feel uneasy because we have no convenient 'form' to latch onto, but our moments of ambivalence—if we manage to relax into them—can allow us to glimpse our nondual nature.

When describing how our capacity for ambivalence reflects our capacity to live the view, Khandro Déchen says: '*The sensation of ambivalence is emptiness. The subject of ambivalence is form. The practice of ambivalence is to allow the two to seamlessly partake of each other.*'

Through openness we begin to get to know ourselves at a level of experience that is amorphous, manifold and in flux. And the more we cultivate our capacity to remain with this, the more we learn to cooperate with the sparkling through of our realised nature.

The following dialogues are the result of what students have experienced through cultivating openness, and through engaging in the practices that foster it. This final chapter, compared to the previous one, may come as good news – practice 'works' in that it leads to the development of greater clarity. The 'hell' of practice can suddenly lighten, and something sparkles through.

Practice and openness is about all those times when the burden of our neuroses suddenly lessens, and we catch glimpses of our beginningless realised nature – or at the very least, how this can be entertained as a possibility.

Editor

Patterning

Apprentice: I seem to be noticing the neurotic patterning of the people around me more than I used to. I realise that I shouldn't judge them, because my goal is to overcome my own neurotic patterning, but I find it frustrating that I can see the neurotic pattern of others and wish I could rid them of it.

Teachers: Noticing others' neurotic patterning is a useful thing, but this does not have to lead to judging them. Their neurotic patterning mirrors their enlightened nature, so open yourself to discovering what is unique and appreciable about them through their patterning. This can be fun. Wishing others to be free of their neurotic patterning is an aspect of compassion. Ultimately, once you realise nonduality and dwell in rigpa,[1] that sense of frustration with others' neuroses is bodhicitta.

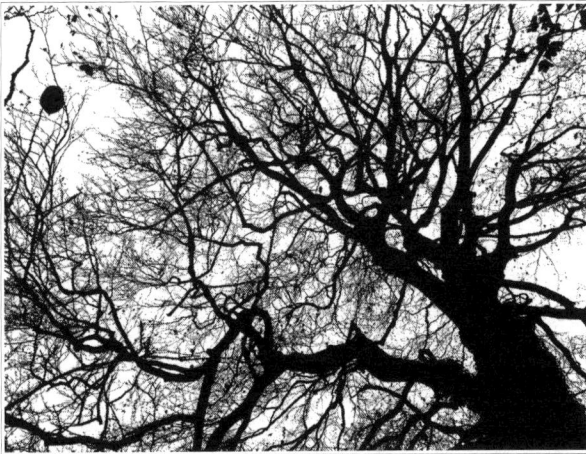

---

1   *rig pa* – the realised experience of the nonduality of emptiness and form, emptiness and bliss.

179

Open delight

Apprentice: Sometimes in practice or teachings I find myself in a clear space in which concepts dissolve and I experience an 'open delight'.

Teachers: 'Open delight' sounds a good space in which to find yourself.

Apprentice: Deliberately bringing about this experience seems impossible though.

Teachers: Yes indeed – you cannot force openness; you can simply create the circumstances in which it can be discovered.

Apprentice: Why do we not realise 'this' all the time? It is all delightfully confusing …

Teachers: Confusion is a great place to start. Once you think you know, then you have fixed your understanding and it is no longer open. Dwelling on why you cannot be present in 'open delight' all the time is not really that useful. Examining 'why' can become hugely distracting and get in the way of practice. The fact is that you are not present in that delightful open space all the time. Having recognised this, you simply continue to engage in the practices that will enable you to continually return there.

Overwhelmed

Apprentice: I feel a sense of wonder and panic arising sometimes when I am meditating. Sometimes it feels a bit unsafe and overwhelming.

Teachers: 'Wonder and panic' sounds pretty good to us – a delightful pairing of emptiness and form words.

You are correct in understanding that there is no safety – but in realising that, you find refuge: the security of no security. If the feeling of being overwhelmed, panicky or scared is getting in the way of meditation practice, switch to a more form-based practice for a while, such as yogic song or sKu-mNyé. If the sense of bewilderment extends beyond the meditation session, engage in down-to-earth activities, such as washing up.

Patterns

Apprentice: It was shocking for me to realise that I only ever contacted you when I was experiencing a crisis. Your comment revealed this pattern, which I had never seen before.

Teachers: It is a fascinating aspect of the teacher/student relationship that a practitioner can have obvious patterns revealed to them and feel astonished that they had never noticed them. We are happy that you are now aware of this pattern, and hope that its revelation was not too uncomfortable for you.

Apprentice: The changes I am experiencing from seeing this pattern are subtle and ongoing.

Teachers: The realisation of this pattern does not mean that you should avoid contacting us when life is not going so well. This could become a 'martyr mode', and as much of a pattern as its opposite. You are always welcome to contact us whenever you wish, and we will always be delighted to hear from you.

The openness of doubt

Apprentice: Once you told me that having doubts about my situation was good, but still I cannot understand why.

Teachers: Doubts about a situation keep it fluid and available for examination – they leave things open. Openness—in terms of being uncertain of an outcome—is an experience of emptiness.

Once you have decided definitely on one side or the other about a situation, then there is no longer openness and the possibility of working with the outcome. Once you have established a concrete view of how the situation should be, there is only the possibility of matters supporting or conflicting with that view. You will encourage and like the things that support it, and hit against the things that oppose it.

This can lead to more judgmentalism and concretising of good and bad, wanted and not wanted, liked and disliked. This tightens the neurotic spiral of judgement and expectation that you are trying to loosen through the opening encouraged by your practice. Allow the doubts to be; allow confusion to flicker; and practice – then you may find that you can be comfortable in a situation of which you are unsure, and engage with it in a fluid and creative manner. Then surprising opportunities may arise from allowing the situation to be open.

Reference points

Apprentice: I understand that reference points are very dangerous, and that makes me sad.

Teachers: It is more helpful to rejoice in the recognition of the pitfalls of referentiality than to become depressed about having reference-points. If you regard your referentiality as 'dangerous' and something to worry about and control, observation becomes like a policeman in the mind.

It is more helpful to have a sense of amusement—rather than telling yourself off—when you notice yourself propping up your sense of self. Otherwise you may become rather serious and lose your spontaneity and sense of humour.

Every time you notice that you are using something as a reference point, this is a spontaneous moment of awareness and something to celebrate. You can laugh at how silly you have been, for example, in getting all worked up about the fact that someone dismissed you as stupid. This might be because you like science fiction, or period drama or soap operas or whatever … . Tantra is intrinsically optimistic, because it recognises the energy of neurosis as no different to the energy of realisation.

Am I ready?

Apprentice: Do you think I am ready to attend this retreat?

Teachers: It was difficult for us to gauge how you were feeling during the retreat with us earlier this year. You were rather quiet and we didn't see you laugh a great deal.

Afterwards you told us that you enjoyed the retreat, so we were content that it had been okay for you. We felt that it was perhaps because it was so new for you and you were shy among the apprentices. However we would like to suggest to you that it is not really possible to sit on the sidelines in the practice of Vajrayana. You have to get in there and get your hands dirty. You can't fashion a clay pot without touching the clay and getting messy. Vajrayana is a direct path and demands the confidence to risk engaging with its directness.

So are you ready to attend this retreat? The only readiness required to attend an apprentice retreat is an open mind, a sense of humour and a willingness to let whatever happens happen. So yes, do come along.

185

Emotional distraction

Apprentice: I realise that my responses are my emotional distraction. To me it is this that is the issue and not the rights or wrongs of any particular case or situation. I recognise that my personal patterning is distraction and response rather than awareness, transformation and clarity in the moment of its energetic arising. This is something that I must keep reminding myself of, be aware of, and be present to.

Teachers: Excellent. This is the best way to respond to having felt wronged or badly treated. Anyone can become emotionally distracted – and recognising this is a critical stage. 'Awareness, transformation and clarity' in the moment are an aspiration – but you cannot live this yet. This is why you practise. Recognising you are not present and aware in the moment *is* practice – so you are doing well.

So near and yet so far

Apprentice: The other day I was struggling with my partner's lapses into hard and angry states of mind and behaviour. Then I suddenly realised that this was a reflection of my own hardness and anger/impatience, and that in fact I was feeling the same way to my partner as they were behaving. I realised that my attitude wasn't helping at all.

Teachers: Well done. This is a real sign of practice. We are delighted. If you can let go of self protection; if you can admit to yourself your sense of vulnerability; if you can let go of the assumption that you know what the person in front of you is feeling or thinking – then you have real opportunities for openness and kindness.

Apprentice: I realised that warmth and openness and love seems to dissolve many unpleasant situations.

Teachers: Yes indeed.

Apprentice: I guess it sounds so simple and straightforward and obvious – but when I saw it, it was lovely.

Teachers: Well in one sense practice is simple, straightforward and obvious – that is why it is difficult. Realisation is so close that it is easy to miss. However moments such as you describe are the moments when it is not missed, and the more you practise the more frequent such moments become.

Emptiness everywhere

Apprentice: I have the feeling that there is a lot of emptiness around me at the moment. Relationships and circumstances do not seem very solid any more. It feels strange seeing things this way, but somehow I'm coming to terms with it.

Teachers: Our lives do seem to go through phases when there is more emptiness in our lives. Everything trundles along nicely for a while and then suddenly everything seems to fall apart. Emptiness happens. Do not read significance into this – it is just what is happening now. Recognising this emptiness and attempting to relax with it is heroic. This is practice.

It is also possible that seeing so much emptiness around you is just a shift in view that has occurred through your practice. This would make it even more important to try to relax into it.

Apprentice: Should I do something to make my relationships more solid, such as calling people more frequently? Sometimes I do this and sometimes I simply leave it as it is.

Teachers: You could try either and see what happens. Meeting and parting are patterns of life. Really close friendships are few in number and such friends will always keep in touch – and if it is not possible to be in touch frequently for periods of time, somehow the sense of closeness remains. If friendships fall away because you are not putting the effort in to maintain them, then perhaps they can simply be allowed to dissolve.

Such friendships may turn out to have been little more than passing acquaintanceships. It may be that the commonality of your lives that created a connection is no longer there.

Shi-nè, every day

Apprentice: I've decided to stop formal self-motivated sitting practice and mantra recitation to focus on remaining with my life experiences as reflections of emptiness.

Teachers: We wonder how this idea arose for you? This may function for a short while if you have engaged in *serious long-term* shi-nè practice, but eventually it is likely that the energy of that practice will be exhausted and you will find that you are losing touch with the capacity to discover emptiness. All practitioners engage in formal practice – it is too easy to kid yourself that you are practising when in fact you are indulging neurosis. We would strongly recommend daily shi-nè practice *as a minimum*. You will find that other practices such as yogic song, mantra accumulation and sKu-mNyé will support the practice of shi-nè. It would also be beneficial to practice dream yoga every night.

Nyam

Apprentice: After our last tsog'khorlo, I had an 'out-of-this-world' experience. After we finished and as I stood up, I had one of the strangest experiences of my life. I was sharp, focused, but somehow not there, and it seemed that there was a large hole in my chest. This experience continued for around 2 hours – though I cannot be sure, as even time seemed to be somehow different. I hope this is not something 'wrong' because all in all I enjoyed the experience – although at the time I had no perception as to whether I was enjoying it or not.

Teachers: This sounds like a most interesting experience. This is called a nyam and is a sign that practice is allowing the psycho-physical elements to relax into their own condition. If one practices meditation, then nyams occur. Nyams manifest through the sphere of the sense fields, so they can be visionary, auditory, olfactory, gustatory, tactile or conceptual. Nyams are not specifically religious experiences and can occur at any time of disorientation. They can be pleasant, unpleasant or strange.

In our experience, they are more likely to occur during retreat, and in the presence of one's teachers. The important thing about nyams is not to seek them out or become attached to them. If a nyam occurs then do not judge or conceptualise about it, and when it diminishes and disappears let it go. Nyam is a side-effect of practice and not the purpose of practice. Do not look for the nyam again or try to recreate it, because the practice of nyam-seeking is not meditation.

Noun or verb

Apprentice: If Tantra is continuity does this mean that 'Tantra' is not a noun – it is not an object and has no form?

Teachers: Tantra is as much a noun as 'dance' is a noun. It describes something that is also a verb. It describes something whose essence is movement and flow and cannot be fixed in form any more than you can fix the continual flow of changing patterns and movements of dance. Tantra is the continuity of existence and non-existence.

Fear of the dark

Apprentice: I am afraid of the dark. I always have to have a night light on in my bedroom and do not like going out at night where there is no street lighting. I feel a little embarrassed about this and feel I should have grown out of it by now

Teachers: You could distract yourself from the fear and dissolve its energy through singing Yeshé Tsogyel mantra, for example – or Dorje Tsig Dün.

It is important however, to remember that practice is not therapy and so practice will not necessarily immediately make the experience of fear more comfortable or easier to cope with. Your relationship with your fear of the dark will certainly change through practice, but it may not disappear or suddenly cease to be a problem. Fear of the dark is an aspect of who you are, and who you are will change through committed long-term practice. Consequently this fear will also change over time.

Dharma is not a 'quick fix' for things that bother you in your life, but having a strong emotion such as this does provide ample opportunity for practice. With regard to growing out of it, this is not necessarily relevant. We do not automatically become grown up—in the sense of losing all childhood fears—once we become physically grown up. Be sensitive to your anxieties and kind with yourself, whilst maintaining a warrior's attitude of a willingness to embrace the fear and work with it.

Transmission at the beach

Apprentice: I wanted to thank you for the teachings that were given at the beach. It is quite extraordinary to me that there are so many different aspects to the teachings and so many ways in which they can be transmitted. It has helped me realise that realisation is possible any time, anywhere, doing anything.

Teachers: We are so glad that the retreat was enjoyable for you and that you had this experience. Practising on the beach seems to have been inspiring for a number of people. You are quite correct that transmission can be experienced and realisation can arise at any time and anywhere.

Apprentice: This felt like such a contrast to how my life as a practitioner usually is. My meditation practice is good, but in ordinary life I feel as though I am watching myself all the time and feel disconnected from others. At the beach, it all seemed so clear and simple and there didn't seem any need for the struggle I habitually seem to experience.

Teachers: To live the view, you have to take the risk of opening yourself to whatever is happening, and to whatever your environment is offering. You cannot hold onto the experience of your meditation practice, trying to keep it close and alive all the time for fear of losing it – such constriction is death to awareness. Meditation experience will filter through into your daily life if you have the confidence to relax and allow it to. Have confidence in your practice and you will find that you can let go of watching yourself and relax.

With relaxation the need to be mindful dissolves because the lived experience of each moment is as it is, and you can then experience as it is as transmission and realisation.

There are things that you can try to remember: openness – avoiding categorising your experience to create reference points; appreciation – recognising the possibility of being happy with whatever is happening; and keeping the sense fields open – so that you are alive in the moment. Of course there will be many moments when you forget and lose your awareness – but there is no need to be hard on yourself when this happens.

The fact that you are noticing it is something to celebrate and is a result of practice. When you notice a prejudice or a pattern of behaviour clicking in automatically, this could start to amuse you. Even when awareness fails you know what it means to be kind, so you can simply be kind.

When is a dog…?

Apprentice: I practice and am committed, but I don't really understand what it is I'm aiming for. What is enlightenment and how can I know whether I am making progress? Is continuing without understanding right effort? Sometimes I feel I should forget all about enlightenment and just try to be kind and aware.

Teachers: Unenlightenment is a bit like thinking you are a dog and trying to be a human being, when in fact you already are human. Others can see that you are human—it is obvious to them—and cannot understand how you think you are a dog. You need to let go of dog-ness and discover that you are human. The effort—to continue the analogy—is to not dwell or wallow in dog-ness, but believe in the possibility of being human. Practise being human by trying to walk on two legs and visualising not being furry. This is a method until you actually discover that you are human. In that instant there can be no method, only realisation. If you then continue with the method, you will lose the moment of realisation. The knack is to discover, to be confident in the discovery, and to allow yourself to remain there effortlessly. At this point you have the paradox of effort and no effort. There is the need to remain, which implies effort, yet it also has to be effortless, or else the effort itself becomes a hindrance. Effort in this sense is maintaining presence.

Forgetting about enlightenment and just being kind and aware is actually an excellent idea – because … what would be the difference between that and enlightenment?

Struggling

Apprentice: I have come to realise how stressed I have caused myself to become by being obsessed with how much rest and sleep I felt I needed. I have discovered that in fact I need far less rest and sleep than I imagined.

Teachers: There can be a tendency to allow opinions and expectations to rule behaviour. If you decide that you need such and such to be happy or well, you may then decide that you must therefore be unhappy or unwell when that is not possible. The stress or tension that you experience in your life can often be simply the result of struggling when you need to relax.

Apprentice: I think that I am starting to accept myself as I am, and learning to rest lightly in that state of awareness.

Teachers: That is wonderful.

Am I there yet?

Apprentice: What is meant by 'the dance of existence and non-existence'. Is this the same as saying that there is only the present, and that the past and future are empty?

Teachers: It is a reference to emptiness and form. You are the dance of existence and non-existence in the sense of your experience of yourself constantly changing, continually arising and dissolving.

Yes, the past and future are empty. They do not exist except as memory and projection. They do not exist in the present moment. Only the present moment exists. Your awareness of the moment that is the present moment can gradually become smaller and smaller as you practice.

Apprentice: Would it be true to say that practice is also like that: that you are either doing it or not doing it in the moment – that you can't say 'I'm working up to it?'

Teachers: Yes ... but that would be a quite an ultimate statement. Chö—Dharma—means *as it is.* Life and practice are as they are. They are perfect and enlightened as they are – you just have to practise in order to know this. You have to learn to allow yourself to stop trying to manipulate and control experience, so that you can discover presence and awareness.

Apprentice: How do you know if you are becoming in any way more enlightened unless you judge your experiences against the indications that you are not enlightened?

Teachers: In one sense you could say that all that can be known is the experience of not being enlightened. However enlightenment is everyone's beginningless natural state, so occasionally it sparkles through. Presence and awareness—realisation or enlightenment—are either your experience in the moment, or they are not. It is not possible to be 'more enlightened' or 'less enlightened'. There can be a greater intensity of the sparkling—and that can create the impression of 'more enlightened'—but nonduality is not graduated.

Your mind-moments of awareness may be rather few and far between where you find yourself today, so the frequency of moments of realisation sparkling through may be rather sporadic. However this frequency will increase with practice and you may start to experience moments of intense sparkling.

When such moments of clarity occur, judging will be irrelevant. You can only judge yourself with your deluded, dualistic mind. When presence and awareness arise spontaneously, remain without doubt, and then continue.

If you attempt to judge a moment of *presence and awareness*, then it is no longer a moment of *presence and awareness*. It will have become a dualistic reference-point. So forget about judging whether you are becoming 'more enlightened', and simply remain continually open to the potential of each mind moment being one of *presence and awareness*.

Cup of tea?

Apprentice: What does it mean that the sphere of long-ku[2] is communicative?

Teachers: It communicates the energy of emptiness and form, arising and dissolving. The energetic tension of form arising from and dissolving into emptiness is felt in this sphere of intangible appearance. It communicates this energy – it is impossible not to receive the message of its energy. Even though it is not possible to understand long-ku from the perspective of dualism, its energy can be experienced.

Apprentice: But long-ku is not really a definable separate state, is it?

Teachers: Indeed. It cannot be separated from chö-ku and trülku. They are a theoretical trio, but in fact a unity – ngo-wo-ku.[3] In tantric practice symbolism is used as the means of riding the energetic communication of long-ku in order to experience the nonduality of emptiness and form – and hence the unification of the three spheres. The sphere of vision communicates between that which is seen as separate: emptiness and form. Engaging with long-ku enables there to be a bridge between the apparent polarities of emptiness and form, to entertain confusion about what is form and what is emptiness.

---

2   Long-ku (*Longs sKu*) in Tibetan, Samboghakaya in Sanskrit, is the sphere of energy. Energy arises from empty potentiality—Chö-ku (*chos sKu*) or Dharmakaya—and manifests as Trül-ku (*sPrul sKu*), Nirmanakaya, realised form. As such, Chö-ku, Long-ku and Trül-ku are a description of reality.
3   ngo-wo-ku (*ngo bo sKu*) is also referred to as dorje-ku, the indestructible sphere.

Through symbolic practice the habitual need to categorise and define can blur so that the vibration of definition/lack of definition; continuity/lack of continuity; separate/not separate; permanent/impermanent; solid/insubstantial can be experienced.

Apprentice: So symbolism communicates without fixing that communication? It eases us into direct experience?

Teachers: Yes, that is a useful way of looking at it. Symbols exist in ordinary life. There are symbolic rituals around visitors for example. Your host may say: 'Welcome. Would you like a cup of tea?' They are not necessarily enquiring as to whether their guest is thirsty. It is a symbolic ritual of smoothing the movement into form of the new situation of a visitor arriving. It enables the host and the guest to become comfortable with one another.

Tuning in

Apprentice: I have been practising mantra as much as I can fit in. Sometimes when I am practising I get a little distracted (no surprise there) and realise I have carried on reciting the mantra and counting the beads but have actually been thinking of something else. Then it feels like I have been 'cheating' and that those recitations shouldn't 'count' – but of course, I don't know how many there have been. Often I just stop turning the beads and recite the mantra a few times without counting, while drawing my attention back, then carry on counting. Is this okay?

Teachers: It is extremely honest of you to recognise this and such integrity in your practice will be most beneficial. It could be said however, that if you were actually able to be totally present, totally focused, totally aware in your mantra practice, then you may need to only recite the mantra once to realise the nature of the yidam. It is because of the fact that practitioners get distracted and lack presence and awareness that such a vast number of repetitions of the mantra must be recited.

When you lose concentration in your shi-nè practice and suddenly realise that you have been off on a thought story, this does not negate your period of practice. Do not castigate yourself for being a bad practitioner. Each moment that you realise that you have lost concentration is a moment of re-emerging awareness and a cause for celebration. It is the same with mantra recitation. If you have still been reciting each syllable of the mantra, then simply continue, bringing your concentration back to the presence of the mantra and the yidam.

Usually the physical connection of beads and breath are enough to keep the mantra alive in the mind at some level. Gradually your ability to remain present with the mantra and the yidam will increase.

Apprentice: I also wanted to ask about visualisation. I am in some way able to be aware of visualising the yidam, but I cannot see them as a clear picture in my mind's eye, as I know some people can. Yet there is some sense that I am seeing but it isn't visible.

Teachers: The Anuyoga [4] style of yidam visualisation is more to do with 'feeling' the yidam than with detailed, exact visualisation. A sense of the yidam grows as you recite mantra, and gradually merges with your own sense of self so that you become transparent.

Apprentice: A lot of the time I just recite the mantra and try to 'tune in' – to the mantra and to the yidam.

Teachers: Good.

4   Anuyoga in Sanskrit, jésu naljor (*rJes su rNal 'Byor*) in Tibetan, is the second of the three inner Tantras. It is concerned primarily with transformation through instantaneous self-arising and through the manipulation of the subtle body.

Mystery

Apprentice: I realise that it is an idiosyncrasy of mine to create an air of mystery around me.

Teachers: Idiosyncrasy is fine as an aspect of personality – in fact it is often delightful. However care must be taken to avoid actively cultivating such personality traits as a means of 'dressing' in a definition that feels safe.

This may be a way of evading genuine interaction or it may create confusion in communication with others.

Apprentice: I suspect that I have cultivated a style of persona that helps me when I am feeling vulnerable and finding social interactions challenging. This involves using techniques I have learned that I believe enable me to act 'normally' and in a manner that is appropriate.

Teachers: Everyone uses strategies to some extent—whether or not they are aware of them—but it is not possible to fully engage with the practice of Vajrayana and continue with such strategies. Vajrayana demands that you are real and present in the moment. A strategy separates you from the present moment so that you become an observer of your own interactions. You create a delay to enable you to judge which strategy to use – but this delay is not empty, it is full of concept.

Vajrayana requires the courage to dance with the tension of the moment – of not knowing the *who, what, why* or *how* of that moment. You have to let go of always trying to control yourself and your situation, and leap into the present moment.

Apprentice: I do have a predilection for analysis and planning, but recognise that my analysis can be biased and faulty.

Teachers: The conceptual mind is a powerful tool, but the problem is trying to use it in all situations.

It would be absurd to try to cook dinner with the same tools you used for mending the car that took you to the supermarket; or the same tools that you used to get the food from the supermarket shelf to your home; or the same tools as you will use to eat the food and clear up afterwards.

Strategies arrest the flow of being. Riding the flow of: who or what you are in any moment; what you are receiving through the sense fields in any moment; and engaging with others in that moment; can only be real and rich if strategies are abandoned.

Once you have established your daily practice of shi-nè and have more experience of emptiness, you will find that the need for strategies will gradually dissolve and you will feel less worried about what might be considered 'normal'. You will be able to relax into just being who you are.

Regular practice

Apprentice: My practice is continuing in the same manner as it has been for the past two years: silent sitting twenty minutes every morning, twenty minutes sKu-mNyé every morning and evening, and two thousand mantras every day.

Teachers: It is wonderful to have established such a regular practice. This is something that many people struggle to achieve, so well done. We admire your dedication and commitment. We are interested to ask however, what happens if at the end of twenty minutes of shi-nè you are particularly settled, vibrant and present? Do you just stop because the clock says twenty minutes is up?

We feel that practice—as with all other areas of life—demands a degree of flexibility. There is the need of an ability to adjust our regular habit when the situation demands it, else there is the danger that practice lacks presence. It is a particular aspect of your personality that you approach life in a slightly rigid and regimented manner. It might be interesting to experiment with mixing things up a little bit. Sometimes sit for the whole of your morning session and only practise sKu-mNyé in the evening, for example. How would you feel if you varied your practice?

Apprentice: My complications at this time are higher and more demanding but my awareness of them seems to diminish their ability to distract me. Do you think that this is a sign of practice or of unresolved deeper issues that I need to work on?

Teachers: We would say this is a sign of practice.

Apprentice: Because I don't know that, I follow a path of practice without deviation.

Teachers: Perhaps you could be a little bit more confident in yourself as a practitioner. Once you have this confidence, you will be able to relax more, and will not need to be so rigid in your approach. This relaxation will then permeate into your life.

Practice isn't all fluffy

New Apprentice: My reaction to struggling with the retreat seems to me that I was being lazy – that I wanted to feel that I couldn't go on with practice. One of my favourite teenage angst songs by Kurt Cobain says '*I take a comfort in being sad* … ' Is there always something a bit cowardly about feeling attracted to depressed states, I wonder.

Teachers: It is good that you recognise that you avoided the struggle of the retreat, rather than rising to the challenge. Depression lacks energy and lustre and it can be easier to indulge in it than rise above it. Energy and lustre require a degree of courage. This is quite a common reaction to something found to be unexpectedly difficult, but your observation and understanding of it is not so common. This is valuable experience upon which you can build more practice.

New Apprentice: I wonder if you could give me some advice and reassurance about feeling uneasy about certain aspects of practice. I understand that practice isn't all fluffy and I don't mind some discomfort, but I'd like to be productive in my unease rather than relying on my tired old coping mechanisms...

Teachers: Practice excites change and this isn't always comfortable. Practice makes you see yourself in ways that you might prefer not to notice. Which aspects of practice make you feel uneasy, and what is the nature of the feeling of unease?

New Apprentice: I think in general terms the things that make me most uncomfortable are those things that I cannot imagine myself doing. sKu-mNyé in a group would be an example – this doesn't seem to be the sort of thing I would do.

Teachers: Hmmm ... That is interesting. It sounds as though you have a fairly well-defined image of yourself. An important aspect of practice and view is to be open to change, and to discovering unexpected qualities and capacities. Once you liberate your energy, anything becomes possible and within your scope.

New Apprentice: And related to this concern is a kind of background worry that other people couldn't imagine me doing it either. I can almost hear certain friends snorting at the idea... Both of these worries are, I know, silly and I feel a bit embarrassed for thinking like this!

Teachers: Friends—in the ordinary understanding of friendship—tend to support you and share in your neuroses. That is why friends are easy and comfortable to be with. Vajrayana turns all that on its head. The practitioner engages with practice and embraces the experience of discovering who they are experientially rather than who they have come to think they are through upbringing and life circumstances.

The friends you find yourself among in a sangha may be people with whom you would never have considered developing relationships. They may have widely differing opinions, backgrounds and life experience. Your vajra friends encourage you to be real, present and to move beyond conditioned views.

These are the people who will engage in the practice of pure view and we are certain that none of them would have any problem imagining you practising sKu-mNyé. Friends may snort at your involvement initially but they may start to admire you when they see that you are changing and becoming kinder and more open.

However—realistically—it has to be recognised that becoming involved in Buddhist practice and changing can be challenging for friends and family and not all relationships survive the experience. You will have to judge for yourself whether the advantages you discover through practice are of sufficient value for you to tolerate the disapproval or astonishment of your friends.

Solitary retreat

Apprentice: Thank you for the wonderful opportunity for solitary retreat. It was quite intense in retrospect. Nothing happened – in the sense of anything out of the ordinary. I just practised really, and had moments of light and clarity and other moments of dullness and stupidity.

Teachers: Sounds pretty good to us for your first weekend retreat.

Apprentice: The Sunday morning was particularly sluggish. I was practising but my mind was very dull and lacked clarity. I'm bringing this up because it concerns me that if I were to engage in a longer retreat I would become ever more dull as the time progressed.

Teachers: This cannot be assumed. You are not linear in that way. This time was only one full day in retreat. It can take a while longer than that to settle into the retreat experience, and dullness can be one aspect of that settling in. Also the focus for this short retreat was very much on silent sitting and mantra accumulation. A longer retreat would include more physical practice and even sessions of study. These can help keep you alert.

Dullness and distraction are the evasion tactics of conceptual mind. Over a longer period of retreat conceptual mind begins to settle out, and give up the need to either assert itself or sulk. Then you start to develop spacious relaxation and the nature of Mind becomes your sense of presence.

Expectation and disappointment

Apprentice: I'm finding that as I release my conditioned concepts about the direction of my life, work is becoming more enjoyable – dare I say even fulfilling. So continuing to work where I am is not as arduous as it seemed a month ago.

Teachers: Silent sitting gradually allows you to let go of living your life through expectation and disappointment. While expectation exists, you continually wish your life to pan out in a particular form and become frustrated and unhappy when life has its own ideas and circumstances create a different form. Meditation enables these patterns of projection and wilful obduracy to reveal themselves – your patterning becomes transparent. Then you can let go of this patterning and learn to be comfortable in the present moment. Once you are able to live in the moment, the form of your life in that moment becomes available to you simply as the experience of *as it is. As it is* will always be perfect because it is *as it is.* Only striving for experience to be different from *as it is* creates that tension of expectation and disappointment.

If your job is unrewarding or unpleasant however, there is always the possibility of changing employment. We would not encourage anyone to continue in a job that does not suit them. It may be that a change would be beneficial. It is important to realise though, that you take *who you are* with you to that new occupation.

If *who you are* continues to attempt to control *as it is*, then you will soon discover that you are experiencing the same problems of expectation and disappointment as before and only the context has changed. Once *you* change—through silent sitting— the context of your life eventually becomes irrelevant to your state of mind.

Definition

Apprentice: I feel secure when I am in the role of organiser and the person who is relied upon to make sure everything runs smoothly, so I am quite comfortable on open retreats. On apprentice retreats however, I feel less secure and find that I am comparing myself to others.

Teachers: It is useful that you have noticed this. Now that you've seen this you can look at the pattern more closely. It could be a bit of a *eureka moment* for you. The role of organiser of an open retreat has a certain form and people relate to you with a certain definition. At an apprentice retreat there is not this definition—there is more emptiness—and this is less comfortable.

This emptiness and lack of definition that you are experiencing as insecurity and feelings of self-doubt are a response and a pattern. Seeing the pattern is the first stage in being able to let it go.

Allow the emptiness to be there and allow yourself to experience that lack of definition. Shi-nè will gradually make it easier to let go of the need to hang on to definition and allow you to be relaxed in a state of no definition. Definition will arise in the moment: *in charge of cooking this meal; student listening; friend chatting at the dinner table; person responsible for clearing the tables...* Definition arises dependent on the need of the moment.

Specialness

Apprentice: There are many intense moments in my life—connected to sensory experiences—yet somehow I am suspicious that I am waiting for something special to occur. It is the same in meditation. This waiting for something feels like a big obstacle. Could you say something about this?

Teachers: You are correct that this is an obstacle – but probably not such a huge one. Everything that is going to happen is happening. There is nothing to cultivate and nothing to expect. Meditation is getting used to. If some spectacular, amazing vision or experience occurs during your meditation practice – you let it go if you are practising shi-nè, and enter the dimension of the experience if you are practising lhatong.[5]

Hence there is nothing special to wait for. Whatever happens, happens. The specialness is in discovering the reality of each moment. The blueness of the sky. The sensation of warm winter slippers. The icy chill on your face. The extraordinary quality of moonlight. The pleasure of a conversation and communication. The smile of a stranger in the street. All the specialness and wonderfulness of experience you could ever imagine are available to you in each and every moment through direct experience. These are the intense moments connected with the sense fields.

---

5   Lhatong (*lhag mThong*) means 'further vision'. Lhatong is the practice that comes after shi-nè: from the perspective of emptiness, one finds presence of awareness in the dimension of that which moves.

If you strive to discover the special moment it will elude you because you have created a separation from it in the striving. The special moment is happening all the time. All you have to do is learn to relax. But do not worry – relaxation will naturally increase with your practice.

Glossary

anuyoga (Sanskrit)

Jésu Naljor (*rJes su rNal 'byor*) in Tibetan. The second of the three inner Tantras. It is concerned primarily with transformation through instantaneous self-arising and through the manipulation of the subtle body.

bodhicitta (Sanskrit)

Chang-chub-sem (*byang chub sems*) in Tibetan. Active compassion, the energy of the enlightened state.

bodhisattva (Sanskrit)

Chang-chub-sempa (*byang chub sems dPa'*) in Tibetan. One who has bodhi – the compassionate mind of enlightenment.

Buddha (Sanskrit)

Sang-gyé (*sang rGyas*) in Tibetan. Complete open wakefulness. The state of enlightenment.

daka (Sanskrit)

Pa'wo (*dPa' bo*) in Tibetan. Hero or warrior.

dakini (Sanskrit)

Khandro (*mKha' 'gro*) in Tibetan. Literally 'sky going lady'; or poetically, 'sky dancer'. Female awareness beings who manifest the functions of the Buddha-karmas, the activities of the realised state. 'Khandro' is a contraction of khandroma (female) or khandropa (male), but is more commonly used to refer to khandroma (*mKha' 'gro ma*).

dams ngag (*gDams ngag*) (Tibetan)

Heart advice.

Dharma (Sanskrit)

Chö (*chos*) in Tibetan. 'As it is', reality, suchness, the way things really are.

dharmakaya (Sanskrit)

Chö-ku (*chos sKu*) in Tibetan. The sphere of unconditioned potentiality or emptiness.

Dzogchen (*rDzogs pa chen po*) (Tibetan)

Mahasandhi in Sanskrit. 'Great completeness', 'utter totality'. The path of spontaneity.

empowerment

Wang (*dBang*) in Tibetan. Tantric transmission into the practice of a yidam.

Four Noble Truths

The first teaching Shakyamuni Buddha gave after fully realising the nondual state. 1. the truth of unsatisfactoriness; 2. the truth of the cause of unsatisfactoriness; 3. the truth of the cessation of unsatisfactoriness; 4. the truth of the path to the cessation of unsatisfactoriness.

gö kar chang lo (*gos dkar lCang lo*) (Tibetan)

Literally 'white clothes, long hair'. The non-celibate yogic sangha that Padmasambhava and Yeshé Tsogyel founded alongside the red, or monastic, sangha.

Guru (Sanskrit)

Lama (*bLa ma*) in Tibetan. The Tantric teacher. Vajra Master.

khandro-pawo nyid-da mélong gyüd

(*mKha' 'gro dPa' bo nyi zLa me long rGyud*) (Tibetan) A teaching where romantic relationship becomes a spiritual practice.

ku-mNyé (*sKu mNye*) (Tibetan)

A cycle of psycho physical exercises that work with the rTsa rLung system. sKu-mNyé literally means 'massage (mNyé) of the subtle body (sKu)'.**kyil'khor** (*dKyil 'khor*) (Tibetan) Mandala in Sanskrit. Literally 'centre and periphery'.

lha-tong (*lhag mThong*) (Tibetan)

'Clarity' or 'further seeing'. One of the two main aspects of the practice of meditation.

Ma-gÇig Labdrön (*Ma gCig Lap sGron*)

A great Tibetan yogini, who was the originator of the practice of gÇöd (often transcribed as 'chöd'). In the Aro gTér Lineage, one of the practices of Lama'i Naljor (Guru Yoga – unification with the mind of the Lama) is connected to Ma-gÇig Labdrön (1055-1145).

mantra (Sanskrit)

Ngak *(sNgags)* in Tibetan. Awareness spell or mantra. Ngak is a method through which we enter into the dimension of vision through the sonic dimension of the awareness being.

ngakma (*sNgags ma*) (Tibetan)

Mantrini in Sanskrit. A female ordained, non-celibate practitioner who holds the Vajrayana vows.

ngakpa (*sNgags pa*) (Tibetan)

Mantrika in Sanskrit. A male ordained, non-celibate practitioner who holds the Vajrayana vows.

nirmanakaya (Sanskrit)

Trül-ku (*sPrul sKu*) in Tibetan. The sphere of realised manifestation.

nirvana (Sanskrit)

State of perfection. Often understood as the opposite of samsara. However in the realm of realisation there is neither samsara or nirvana. From the perspective of Dzogchen, samsara and nirvana as different states is a dualistic concept.

nyam *(nyams)* (Tibetan)

Meditational experiences that result from practice. Nyams should not be sought out.

Nyingma (*rNying ma*) (Tibetan)

> 'Ancient' or 'old translation' lineage. The oldest form of Buddhism in Tibet, founded by Padmasambhava and Yeshé Tsogyel.

Padmasambhava (Sanskrit)

> Pemajungne (*Padma 'byung gNas*) in Tibetan. 'Lotus-born'. The Tantric Buddha. Also known as Guru Rinpoche.

pa'mo (*dPa' mo*) (Tibetan)

> Heroine or warrior. A female practitioner that has discovered her inner pawo (daka) and who manifests it externally through enlightened activities that benefit others.

rigpa *(rig pa)* (Tibetan)

> The realised experience of the nonduality of emptiness and form, emptiness and bliss.

sambhogakaya (Sanskrit)

> long-ku (*longs sKu*) in Tibetan. The sphere of intangible appearance, vision, realised energy.

samsara (Sanskrit)

> khor-wa (*'khor ba*) in Tibetan. Literally 'going around in circles'. The cyclic experience of being. The state in which every activity undermines itself in terms of our attempt to establish ourselves as being solid, permanent, separate, continuous and defined.

sangha (Sanskrit)

> gendün (*dGe 'dun*) in Tibetan. The community of practitioners.

sem *(sems)* (Tibetan)

Mind with a small 'm' – mind that drifts into dualism and which attempts to prove that it is solid, permanent, separate, continuous and defined. As distinct from sem-nyid *(sems nyid)*, the Nature of Mind. Sem-nyid is the empty quality of Mind and space of awareness in which sem (small 'm' mind) manifests and can either enter into compassionate communication or lose itself in dualistic manipulation.

seven line song

Dorje Tsig-dün *(rDo je tshig bDun)* in Tibetan. The Seven Thunderbolt Phrases of Padmasambhava.

shi-nè *(zhi gNas)* (Tibetan)

The practice of silent sitting. Remaining uninvolved with the thought process.

siddhi (Sanskrit)

Ngödrüp *(dNgos grub)* in Tibetan. Accomplishment. Usually refers to the ultimate siddhi of enlightenment, or to the relative siddhis which are miraculous powers.

skandhas (Sanskrit)

The sutric analysis of perception, the five mental aggregates.

svabhavikakaya (Sanskrit)

Dorje-ku *(rDo rJe sKu)* in Tibetan. The indestructible sphere of being. Essential indivisible sphere of being. Also known as ngo-wo-ku *(ngo bo sKu)*.

Tantra (Sanskrit)

Gyüd *(rGyud)* in Tibetan. Literally 'thread' or 'continuity'. The teachings of Buddhism which have as their basis the principle of transformation.

tantrika (Sanskrit)

gyüdpa *(rGyud pa)* in Tibetan. A practitioner of Tantra.

teng'ar (*phreng 'a*) (Tibetan)

Mala in Sanskrit. A rosary used for counting mantra recitations.

tér (*gTér*) (Tibetan)

An abbreviation gTérma. Teachings, practices and objects hidden by Padmasambhava and Yeshé Tsogyel for the benefit of future disciples and the regeneration of Tantric lineages.

tsa lung (*rTsa rLung*) (Tibetan)

The subtle energetic body that is engaged in yogic practices.

vajra (Sanskrit)

Dorje *(rDo rJe)* in Tibetan. Thunderbolt, diamond. That which is of the nature of realisation: vajra body or vajra nature. Literally 'lord stone'. Used as an adjective the word conveys the idea of invincibility and indestructible form.

vajra master

Dorje lopön (*rDo rJe bLo dPon*) in Tibetan, vajracharya in Sanskrit. The empowering Lama with whom the disciple holds vows.

Vajrayana (Sanskrit)

Dorje Thegpa *(rDo rJe theg pa)* in Tibetan. The six Tantric vehicles of the nine vehicles of the Nyingma School. The teachings of Buddhism which have as their basis the principle of transformation.

Yeshé Tsogyel (*ye shes mTsho rGyal*)

Khandro Chenmo Yeshé Tsogyel. The consort of Padmasambhava. The female Tantric Buddha.

yidam (*yid dam*) (Tibetan)

Deva in Sanskrit. Awareness being.

yogi / yogini (Sanskrit)

Naljorpa (*rNal 'byor pa*) / naljorma (*rNal 'byor ma*) in Tibetan). Male and female practitioners of Tantra. Those who rest in the natural state.